VOCABULARY MAGIC

illustrated by Patty Pangle

Imogene Forte

Mary Ann Pangle

Cover by Cynthia Crook

Copyright © 1977 by Incentive Publications, Inc. All rights reserved. No part of this publication may be reproduced, stored in a retrieval system, or transmitted, in any form or by any means, electronic, mechanical, photocopying, recording, or otherwise, without prior written permission of Incentive Publications, except as noted below.

All student activity pages are designed to be used by individual pupils. Permission is hereby granted to the purchaser of one copy of Vocabulary Magic to reproduce copies of these pages in sufficient quantity for use by the students in one classroom.

ISBN 0-913916-49-8
Library of Congress Catalog Card Number 77-89526

Printed in Nashville, Tennessee
United States of America

TABLE OF CONTENTS

Vocabulary Games

Alphabetical Action...(word usage)	8
Antonym Tennis...(antonyms)	10
Be A Ringer...(word recognition)	12
The Big Race...(word recognition and meaning)	14
Buried Treasure...(word usage)	16
Category Canyon...(categorization)	18
Changing Letters...(homonyms)	20
Communicade...(word meaning)	22
Compound Cards...(compound words)	24
Contraction Course...(contractions)	26
Dictionary Dominoes...(dictionary usage)	28
Dizzy Descriptions...(descriptive words)	30
Ecologically Speaking...(word meaning)	32
Footprints...(word meaning)	34
Geography Gamble...(vocabulary extension)	36
Know Your Nouns...(functional word usage)	38
Mastering Obstacles...(word meaning)	40
Metric Toss...(vocabulary extension)	42
Paper Planes...(functional word usage)	44
Pick A Pair...(vocabulary extension)	46
Prefix Profile...(word usage)	48
Right Direction...(word usage)	50
Slinky Sections...(word usage)	52
Special Mail...(word meanings)	54
Super Synonym...(synonyms)	56
Take A Nibble...(vocabulary extension)	58
Travel Tips...(functional word usage)	60
Word Walk...(vocabulary extension)	62

Skills Development Activities

- Alphabet Junction...(vocabulary extension) 67
- Contraction Comedian...(contractions) 71
- Fun House...(word meaning) 75
- Jaunty Jargon...(contemporary word usage) 79
- Picture Premium...(word meaning for beginning readers) 83
- Prefix Preview...(prefixes) 87
- Sea Breeze...(compound words) 91
- Synonym Sample...(synonyms) 95
- Valuable Values...(functional word meaning) 99
- Wonderful Words...(multiple meanings) 103
- Word Foolers...(word usage) 107

VOCABULARY MAGIC

Vocabulary Magic is composed of games, game boards, individual and group experiences and reproducible student activity sheets to provide motivation and extension of basic vocabulary skills. All of the activities are based on topics of high interest to boys and girls today and feature functional contemporary vocabulary usage. Complete and easy-to-follow directions for both teachers and students accompany each activity. To provide for optimum flexibility, the format and presentation of content in all of the activities have been kept simple and open-ended. Many of the games and game boards are easily adaptable to other subject areas such as math, social studies or science. The reproducible activity sheets have been organized with a common title around a single skills area to facilitate either a learning center or a unit approach.

The activities have been planned to meet the needs and interests of students with differing abilities and interests, and to be implemented in a variety of classroom settings. Their use is not limited to open space, traditional or any other organizational arrangement. Many of them are adaptable for use with the entire class; others are designed for a small group, and some may be enjoyed by an individual student.

<u>Vocabulary Magic</u> is much more, however, than a collection of "fun and games" activities. The book's major purpose is to encourage the use of vocabulary skills in a relaxed and meaningful setting, and to allow students to become personally involved in spontaneous learning experiences. Game boards, student activity pages and supportive materials have been designed to be easily produced, stored and implemented. The materials necessary for their construction have been limited to those readily available in most classrooms and call for no special artistic ability. In many instances, students themselves will want to become involved in the selection and preparation of activities most appropriate for use in their own classrooms.

We hope that this collection will bring a spark of **VOCABULARY MAGIC** to teachers and students who use it.

Imogene Forte
Mary Ann Pangle

Notes

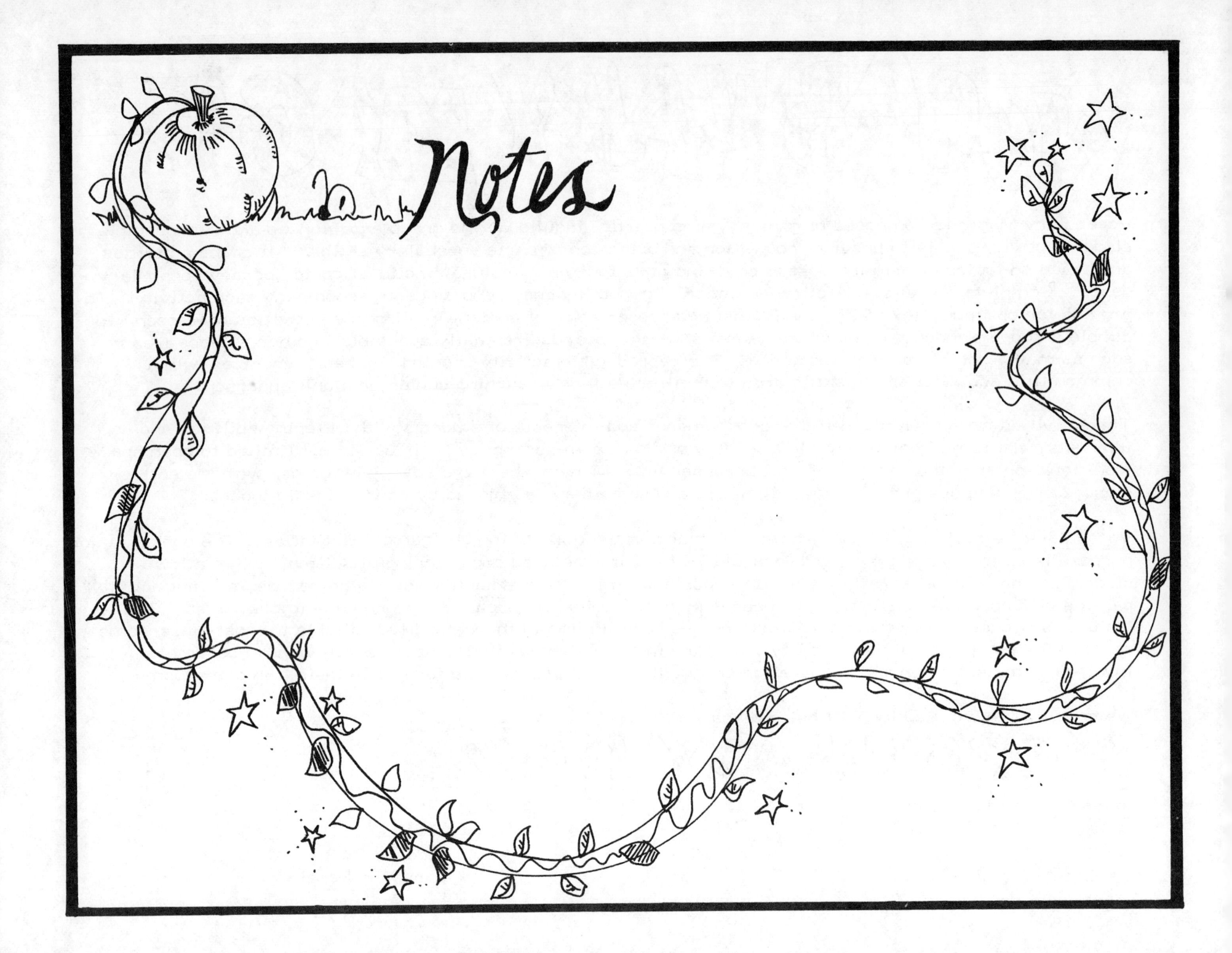

VOCABULARY GAMES

alphabetical action

Preparation Directions:

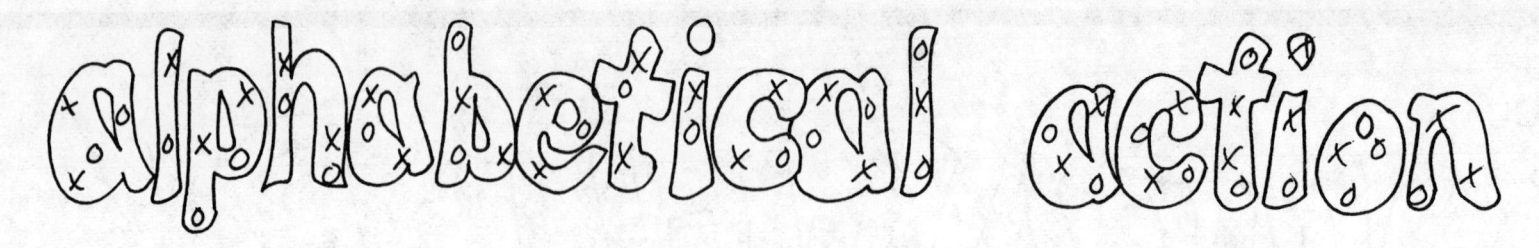

1. Use forty index cards and print three words on each card to be arranged in alphabetical order.

    Example: air
              apple
              ate

2. Provide a chalkboard, chalk, erasers and a small bell.

Player Directions:

1. This relay is for any number of students.

2. The students are divided into two equal teams.

3. The cards are shuffled and divided into two equal stacks.

4. The first student from each group draws one card, skips to the chalkboard and writes in alphabetical order the three words which are written on the card.

5. After the words are written on the board, the student must tag the next member of the team before another card may be drawn.

6. The relay continues until one team has drawn all the cards and has written the words in alphabetical order on the board.

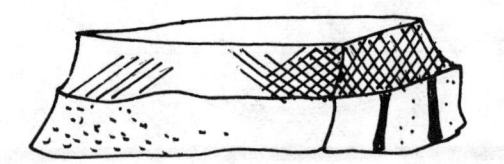

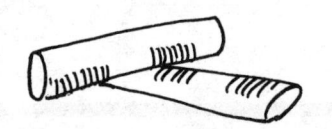

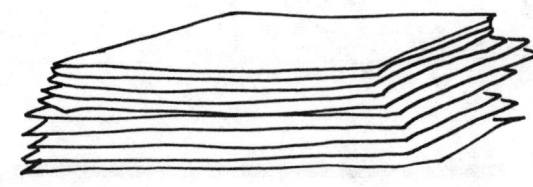

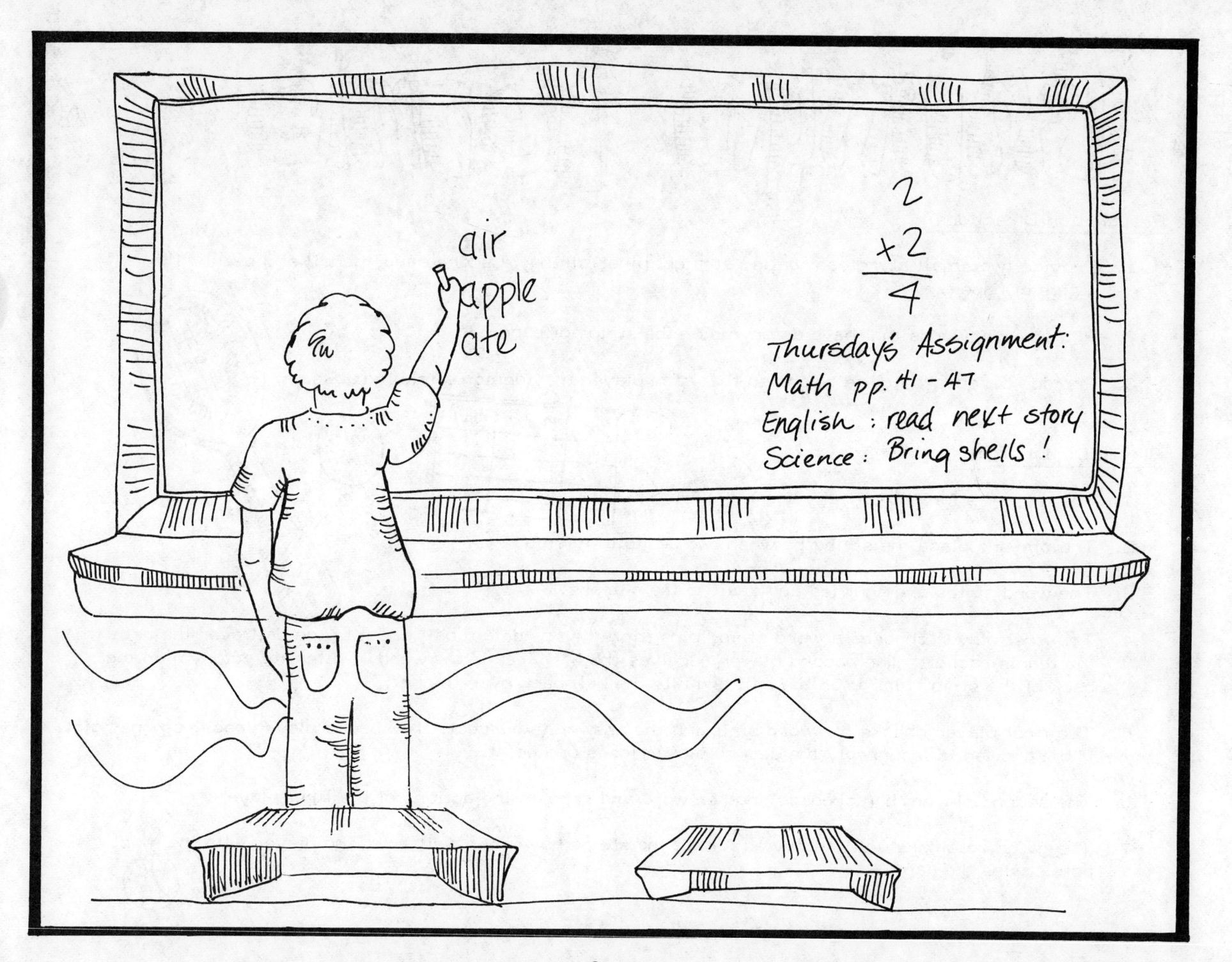

air
apple
ate

$$\begin{array}{r}2\\ \times 2\\ \hline 4\end{array}$$

Thursday's Assignment:
Math pp. 41 - 47
English: read next story
Science: Bring shells!

9

Antonym Tennis

Preparation Directions:

1. Provide two small styrofoam balls, straight pins, string, a score card, pencil and twenty 1" x 2" strips of paper.

2. Print twenty words that have antonyms on the strips of paper.

3. Provide cardboard and felt pens so that each player may design a tennis racket.

Player Directions:

1. This game is for two players.

2. The players place the string between two desks to form a net.

3. The word strips are shuffled and dealt to the players.

4. The first player chooses a word strip, pins it on the styrofoam ball and hits the ball over the net with the tennis racket. The second player receives the ball, reads the word, writes its antonym on the back of the strip, pins it on the ball and hits the ball back over the net.

5. The first player checks the word strip. If the answer is correct, the second player receives one point. If the answer is incorrect, the second player loses one point.

6. The second player then chooses another word and repeats the actions of the first player.

7. The game continues until antonyms for all the strips have been written. The player with the most points wins the game.

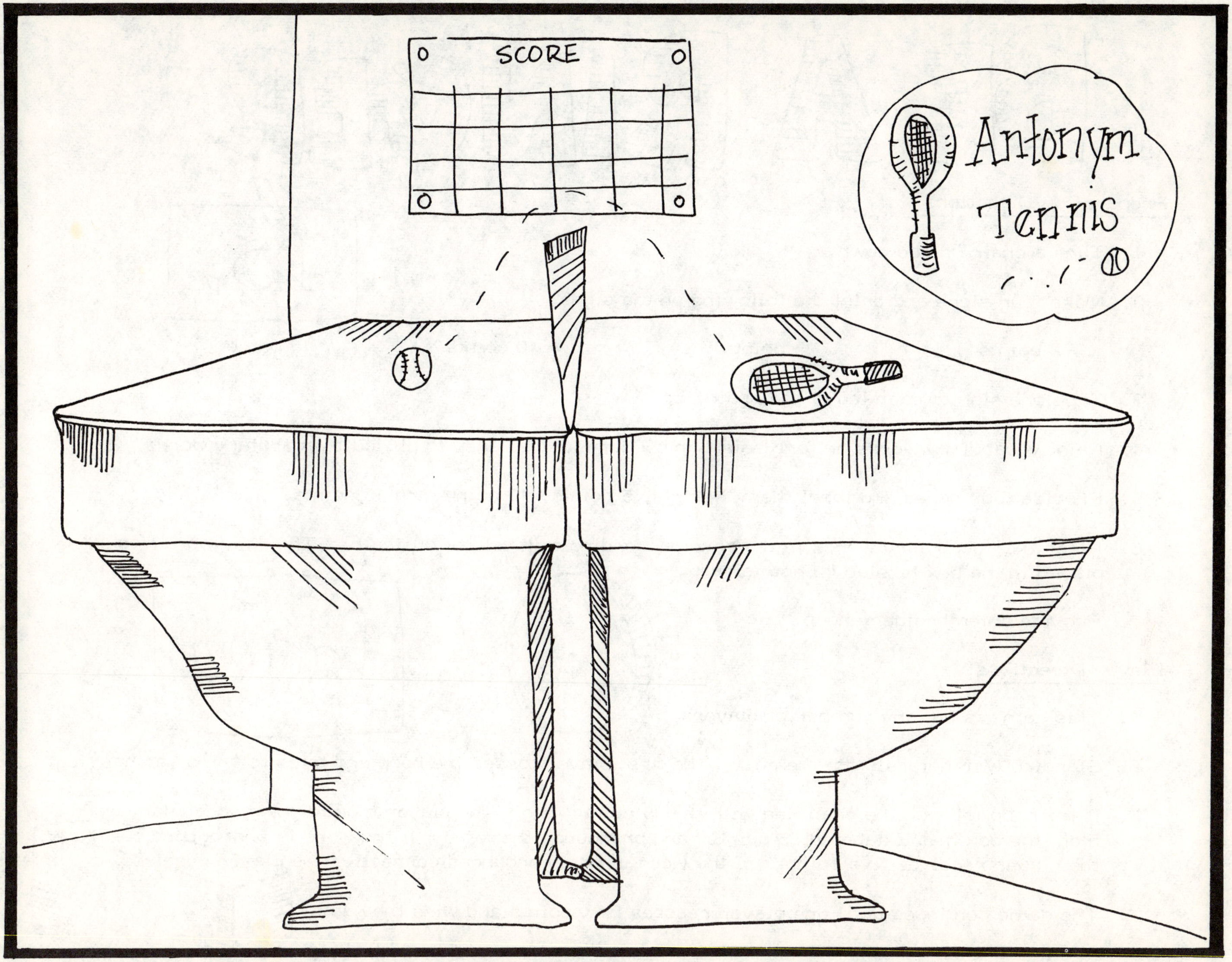
SCORE
Antonym Tennis

BE A RINGER

Preparation Directions:

1. Turn a chair upside down.

2. Make four signs and print the following on the signs:

    2 points   5 points   10 points   15 points

3. Tape one sign to each leg of the chair.

4. Print vocabulary words on forty-eight index cards. Use easy to difficult vocabulary words.

5. Provide four boxes and label them 2 points, 5 points, 10 points and 15 points.

6. Place the vocabulary words in the boxes according to levels of difficulty. The easy words would be placed in the box labeled "2 points" etc.

7. Provide an embroidery hoop.

Player Directions:

1. This game is for any number of players.

2. Standing two meters from the chair, the first player tosses the hoop and tries to "ring" a chair leg.

3. If the hoop falls on the chair leg with the "5 points" sign, the player must draw a vocabulary word from the box that is labeled "5 points" and pronounce the word. If the word is pronounced correctly, the player receives five points. If the word is not pronounced correctly, the player receives no points.

4. The game continues until one player reaches fifty points and wins the game.

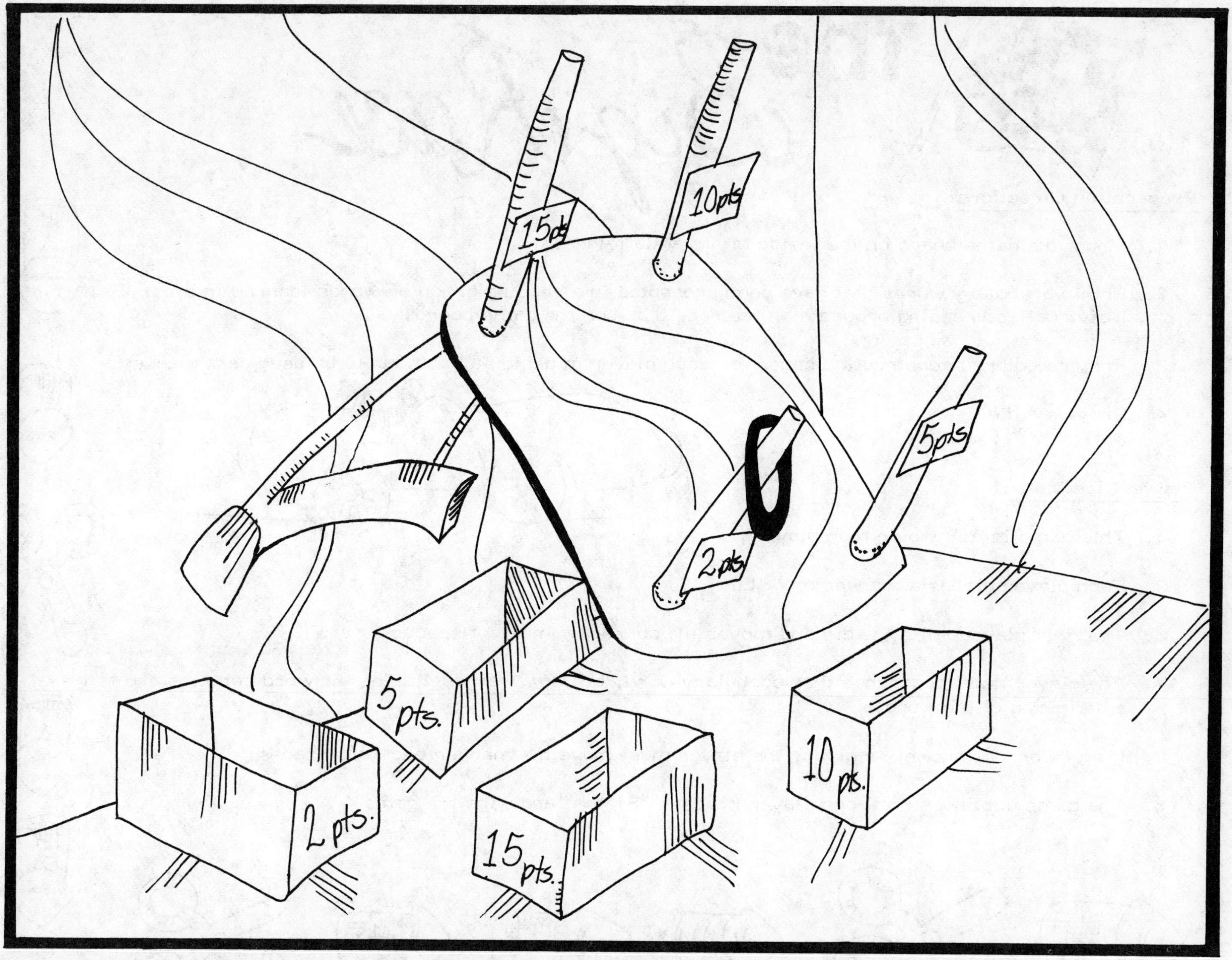
15pts
10pts
5pts
2pts
5 pts.
2 pts.
15pts.
10 pts.

The Big Race

Preparation Directions:

1. Mount the game board on the inside of a manila folder.

2. Print vocabulary words that have been presented in a reading group or words learned in an individualized reading program on the race track on the game board.

3. Provide colored construction paper for each player to design a race car to be used as a marker.

4. Provide a die.

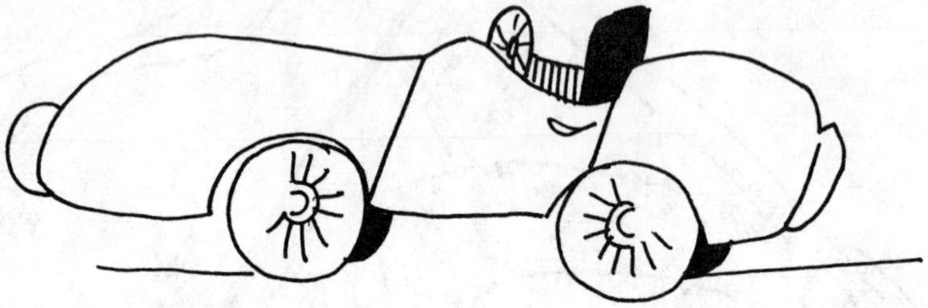

Player Directions:

1. This game is for two or four players.

2. Each player places a marker on "Start."

3. The first player rolls the die and moves the correct number of spaces.

4. The player must pronounce the vocabulary word, tell how many syllables the word contains and tell a definition of the word.

5. If an incorrect answer is given, the player must move the marker back two spaces.

6. The game continues until one player reaches "Finish" and wins the game.

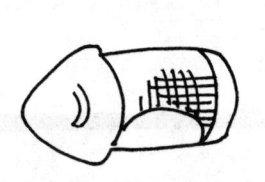

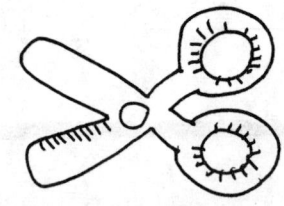

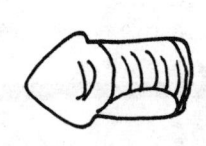

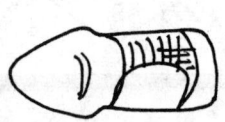

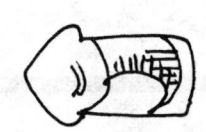

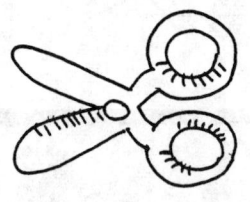

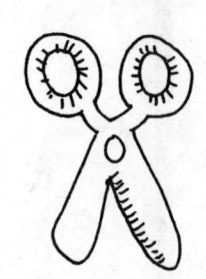

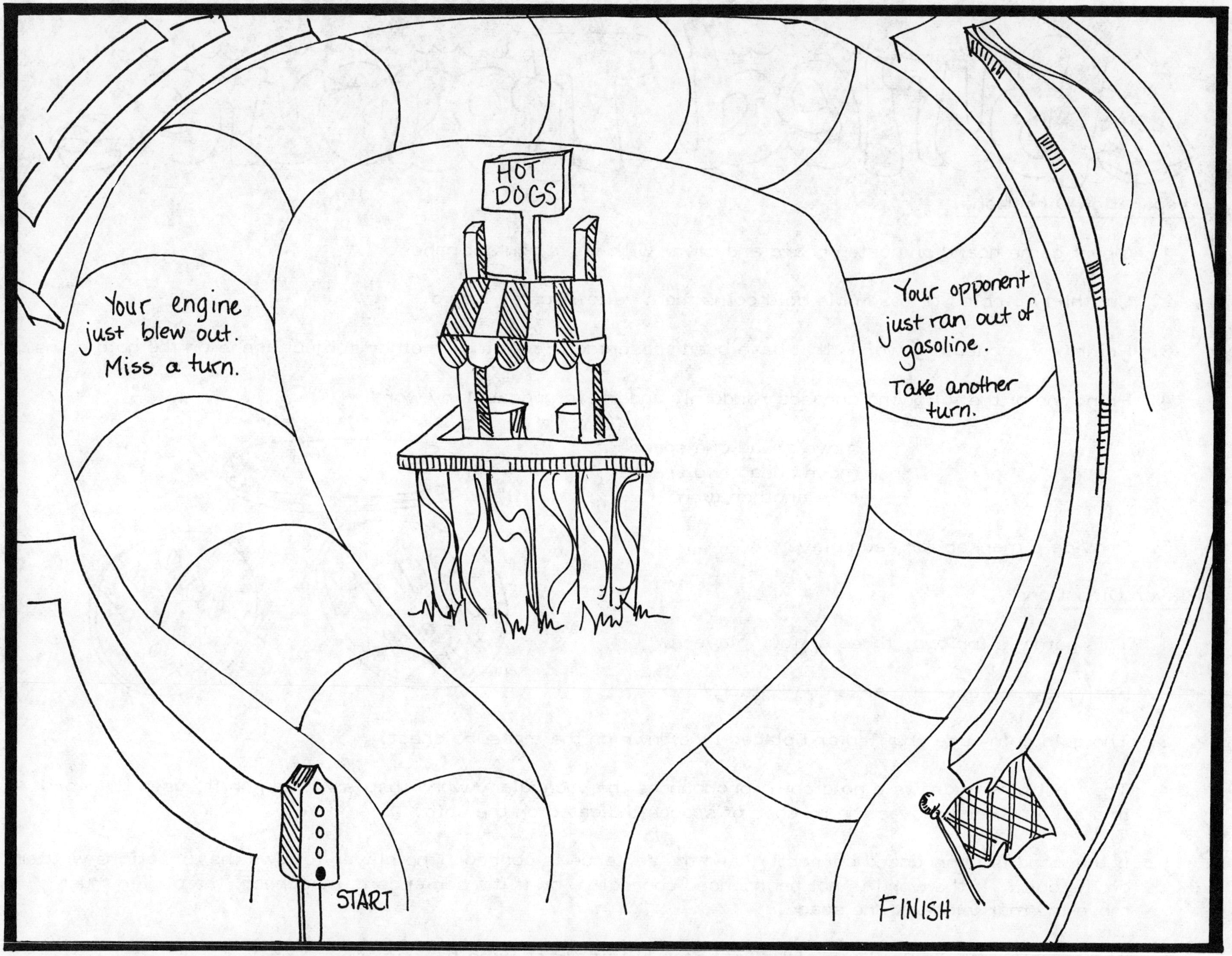
HOT DOGS
Your engine just blew out. Miss a turn.
Your opponent just ran out of gasoline. Take another turn.
START
FINISH

Buried Treasure

Preparation Directions:

1. Mount game board on poster board and cover with clear contact paper.

2. Cut thirty circles to resemble gold coins from yellow poster board.

3. Print new vocabulary words that have been presented in reading or other subject areas on the gold coins.

4. Print one of the following phrases randomly under each vocabulary word:

    > move ahead one space
    > move ahead two spaces
    > take another turn

5. Provide a marker for each player.

Player Directions:

1. This game is for two, three or four players.

2. Each player places a marker on "Start."

3. The gold coins are shuffled and placed face down on the treasure chest.

4. The first player draws a gold coin, pronounces the vocabulary word that is written on it, uses the word in a sentence and moves the number of spaces indicated on the coin.

5. If the word is pronounced correctly, and the sentence is correct, the player follows the directions written on the coin. If the word is not pronounced correctly, or if the sentence is incorrect, the player must move the marker back one space.

6. The game continues until one player reaches "Finish" and wins the game.

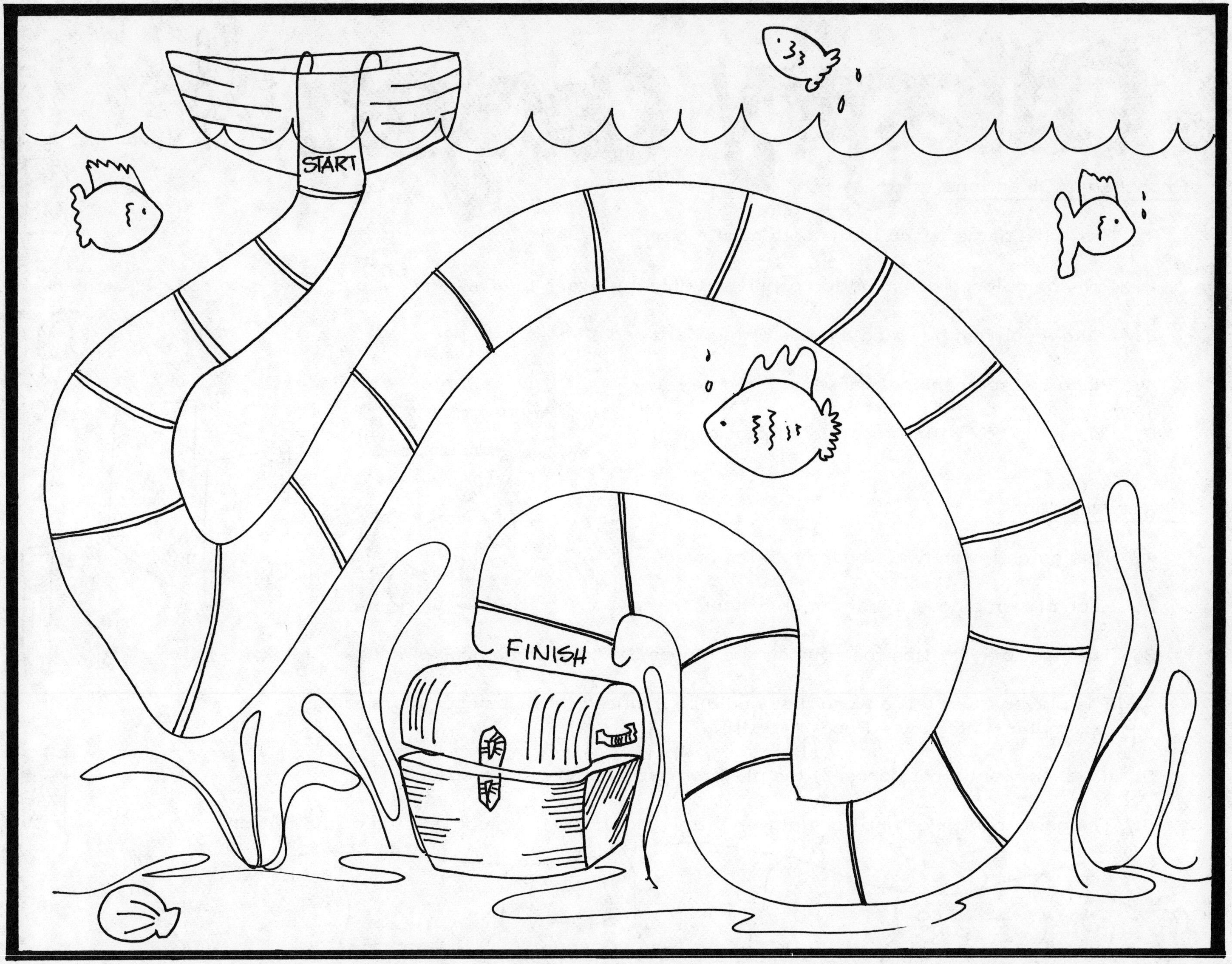
START
FINISH

Category Canyon

Preparation Directions:

1. Paste the game board in the bottom of a box.

2. Provide colored construction paper and direct players to draw and cut out donkeys to be used as markers.

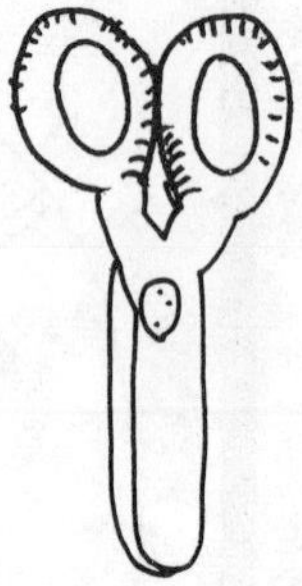

3. Make a spinner by using a piece of tagboard and a brass fastener.

4. Place the spinner and markers in the box.

5. Cover the box with attractive contact paper.

Player Directions:

1. This game is for two, three or four players.

2. Each player places a marker on "Start."

3. The first player flips the spinner and moves the correct number of spaces.

4. The player must tell a word that would be included in the category landed on.
   (Example: Category – Food – Milk)

5. If the answer is not correct, the player must move back one space.

6. The game continues until one player climbs down and up the other side of the canyon.

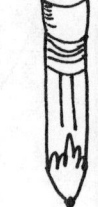

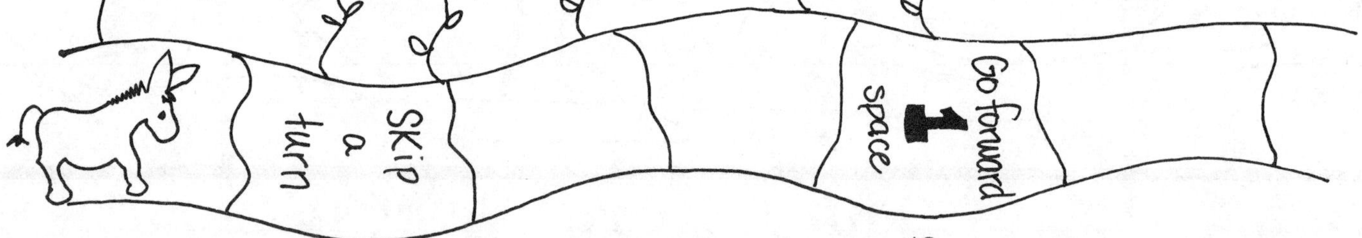

PLAY CATEGORY CANYON

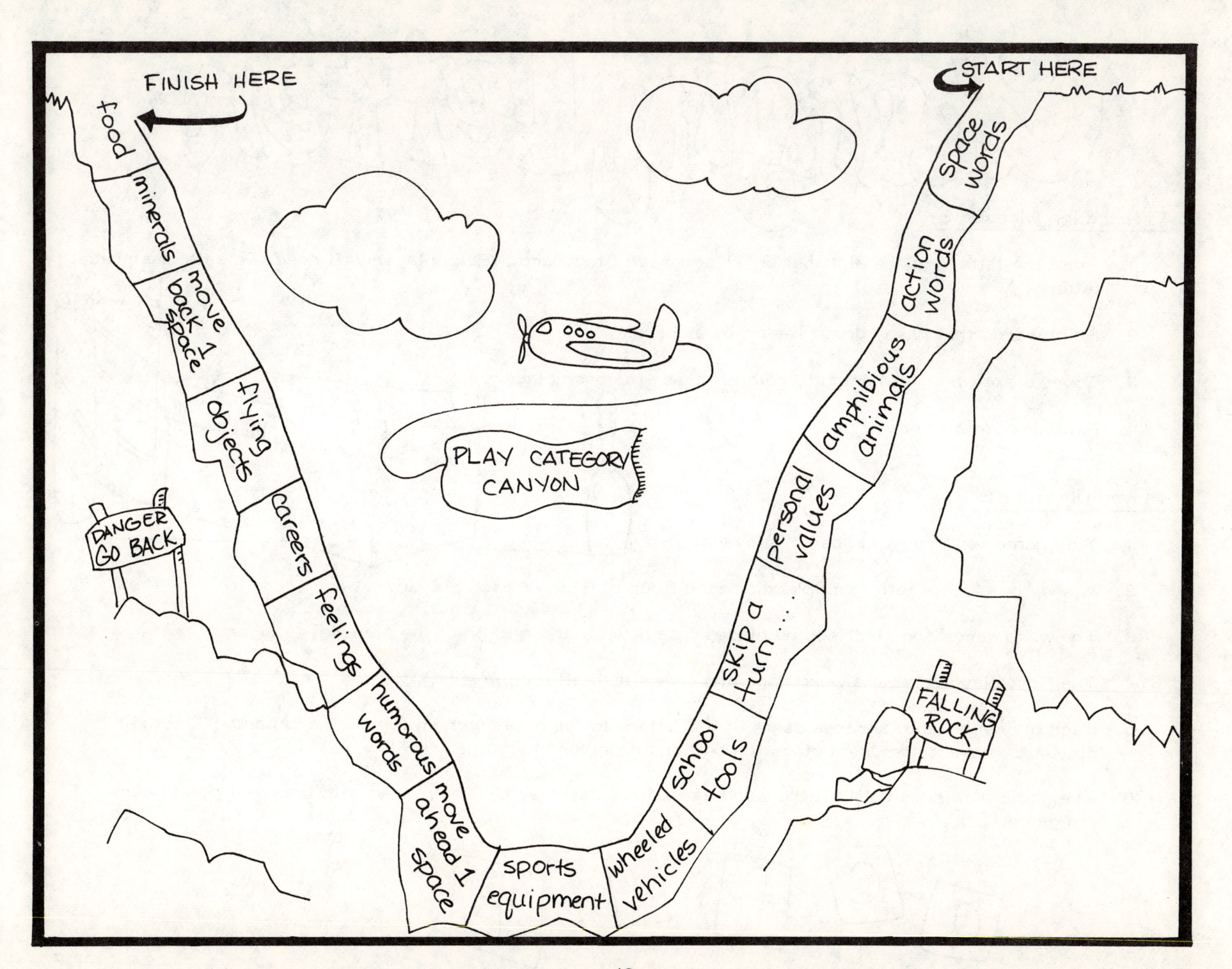

START HERE → space words → action words → amphibious animals → personal values → skip a turn → school tools → wheeled vehicles → sports equipment → move ahead 1 space → humorous words → feelings → careers → flying objects → move back 1 space → minerals → food → **FINISH HERE**

DANGER GO BACK

FALLING ROCK

19

Changing Letters

Preparation Directions:

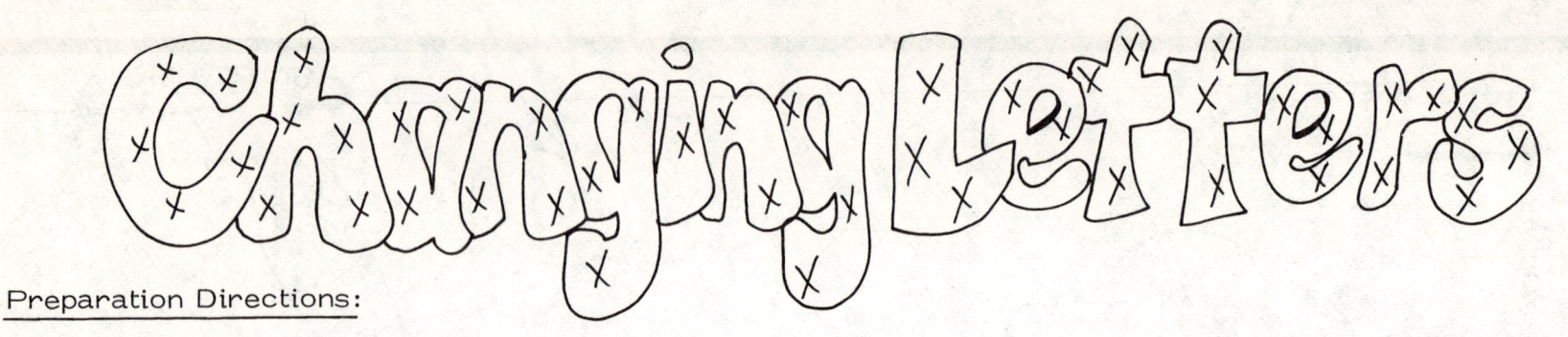

1. Print the letters of the alphabet on 2" squares of tagboard. Each player will need two sets of alphabet letters.

2. Print words that have homonyms on index cards.

3. Cover a shoe box with brightly colored paper for each player.

4. Provide a small bell.

Player Directions:

1. This game is for any number of players.

2. A shoe box full of letters is placed on the floor in front of each player.

3. The word cards are shuffled and placed face down in the middle of the players.

4. The first player draws a word card and shows it to all the players.

5. Each player tries to arrange some of the letters to form a homonym for the word card. The first player to make a homonym rings the bell and receives one point.

6. The game continues until all the word cards have been used. The player with the most points wins the game.

Our Books
The Secret Garden
The Lonely Monster
Changing Letters
Joan
Bob

Communicade

Preparation Directions:

1. Mount the game board on a piece of poster board.

2. Provide a 2" square piece of colored construction paper and felt pens so that each player may make a marker.

3. Ask players to draw one means of communication on the markers.

4. Print the words "Written Communication" on four index cards.
   Print the words "Listening Communication" on four index cards.
   Print the words "Spoken Communication" on four index cards.
   Print the words "Visual Communication" on four index cards.

Player Directions:

1. This game is for any number of players.

2. The word cards are shuffled and placed face down on the game board.

3. Each player places a marker on "Start."

4. The first player draws a card and tells one means of communication that matches the type written on the card.
   Example: written communication – letter
   visual communication – smoke signals

5. If the player gives the correct answer, the marker is moved forward one space. If the answer is incorrect, the marker is moved back one space.

6. The game continues until one player reaches "Finish" and wins the game.

Start

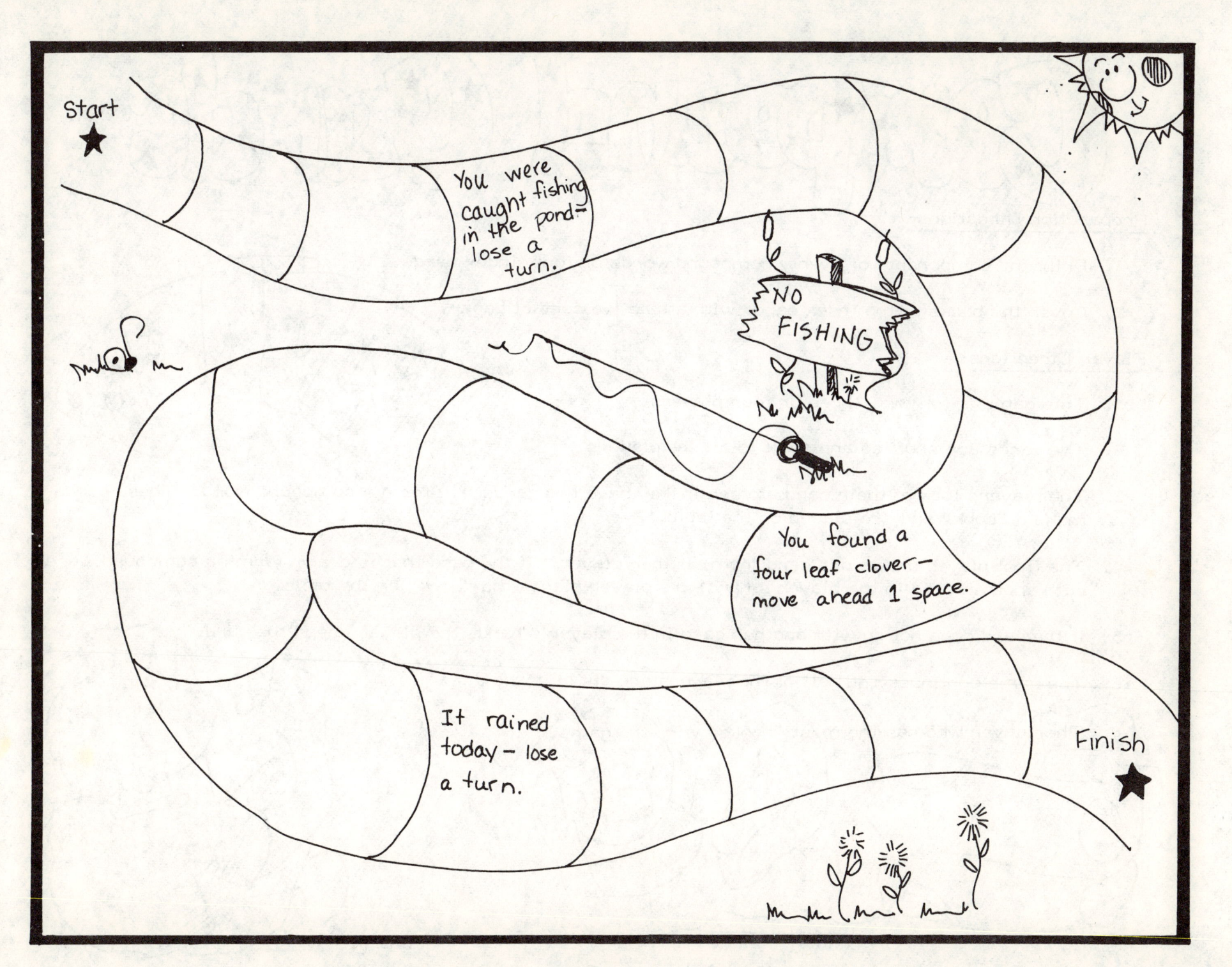

You were caught fishing in the pond— lose a turn.

NO FISHING

You found a four leaf clover— move ahead 1 space.

It rained today— lose a turn.

Finish

Compound Cards

Preparation Directions:

1. Print the components of twenty compound words on forty index cards.

2. Cover the backs of the index cards with attractive contact paper.

Player Directions:

1. This game is for two, three or four players.

2. The cards are shuffled and dealt to all the players.

3. The players look at their cards to see if they have two cards that form a compound word. These cards make a "book" and are placed on the table.

4. The first player draws one card from another player. If the card that is drawn forms a compound word with another card in the player's hand, the player places the "book" on the table.

5. If the card does not go with another card in the player's hand, the player keeps the card.

6. The game continues until all of the players are out of cards.

7. The player who has the most "books" wins the game.

snow	flake	sea	shore

fire	man	sky	rocket

Contraction Course

Preparation Directions:

1. Mount the game board on poster board.

2. Provide an index card for each player to use to make a marker. Direct each student to color and cut out a personal marker in the shape of a golf tee.

3. Provide a die.

Player Directions:

1. This game is for two or four players.

2. Each player places a marker on the first "tee."

3. The first player throws the die and moves the correct number of holes.

4. The player must say and spell a contraction from which the letter or letters printed on the game board space are omitted.

5. If the answer is incorrect, the player loses one turn.

6. The players continue to play until one player reaches the "eighteenth hole." This player wins the game.

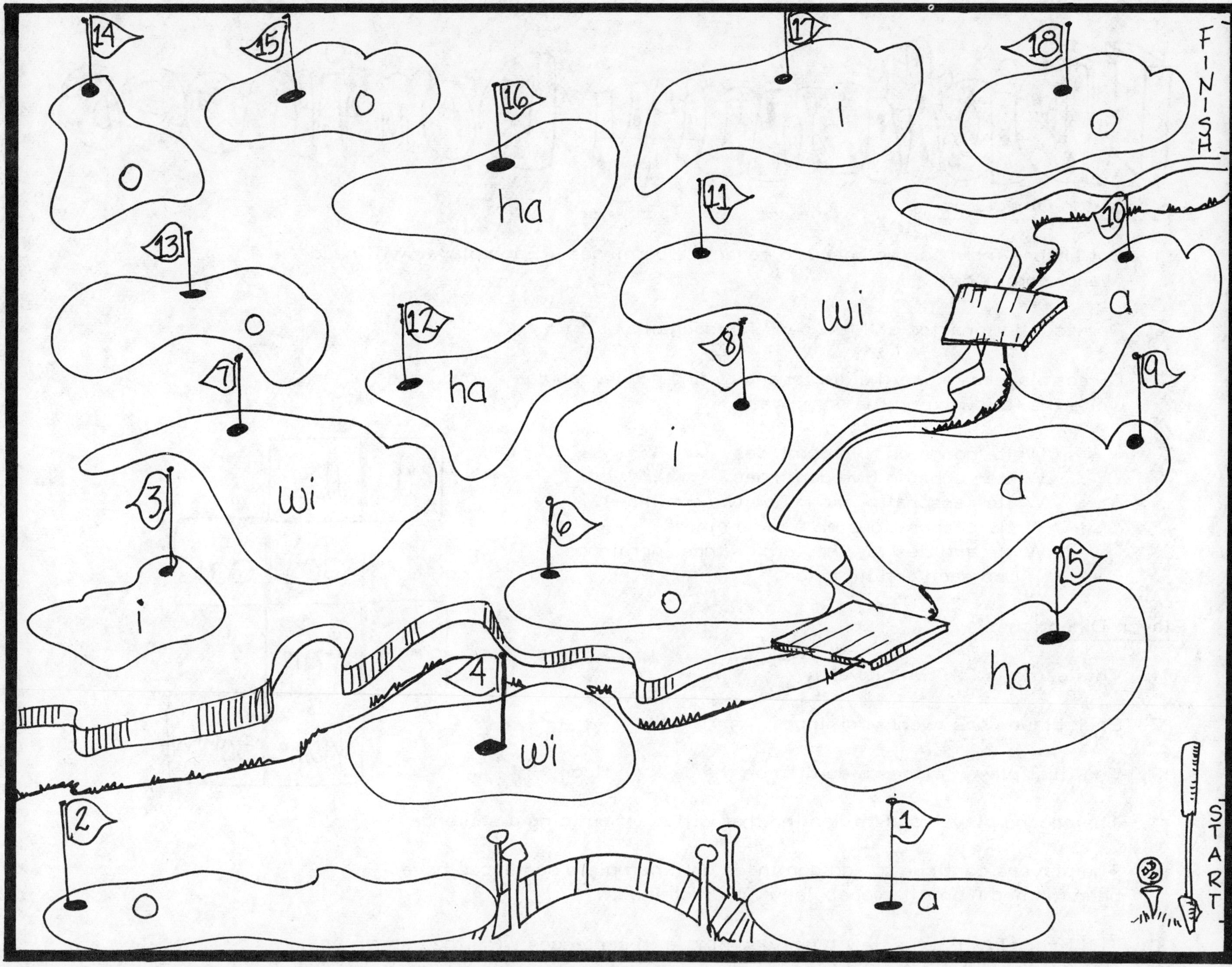
FINISH
14
15
17
18
o
16
o
i
o
ha
11
10
13
wi
a
o
12
8
ha
7
9
i
a
3
wi
6
5
i
o
4
ha
wi
2
1
START
o
a

Dictionary Dominoes

Preparation Directions:

1. Cut shapes from poster board to resemble dominoes. Each player will need twenty dominoes.

2. Provide dictionaries and felt pens for each player.

3. Direct players to use the dictionary to find new vocabulary words and write the following on the dominoes:

    Write nouns on five dominoes.
    Write verbs on five dominoes.
    Write personal pronouns on two dominoes.
    Write prepositions on five dominoes.
    Write articles (a, the, an) on three dominoes.
       Use each article twice.

Player Directions:

1. This game is for two players.

2. Each player has twenty dominoes.

3. The first player places a domino on the desk or floor.

4. The second player adds a domino that will start building a sentence.

5. The players continue to add dominoes until complete sentences have been formed from the vocabulary word dominoes.

6. The first player to use all twenty dominoes in sentences wins the game.

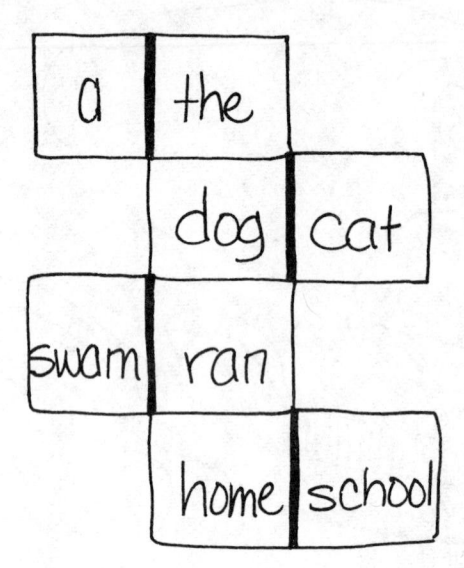

29

Dizzy Descriptions

Preparation Directions:

1. Draw or cut out pictures from magazines of forty objects. Paste the pictures on squares of colored poster board.

2. Place the object cards in a box.

3. Provide a large empty soda pop bottle.

Player Directions:

1. This game is for any number of students.

2. The players sit in a circle on the floor. One student spins the bottle in the middle of the circle.

3. When the bottle stops and is pointing to a particular player, the person in the middle of the circle holds the card box and lets that player draw an object card.

4. The player must name the object and describe how the object looks, tastes, smells or feels and what the object can do.

5. If the correct answers are given, that player becomes the next person to spin the bottle.

6. The game continues until all of the object cards have been used.

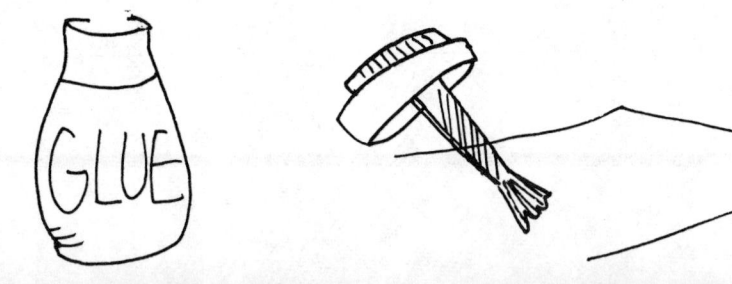

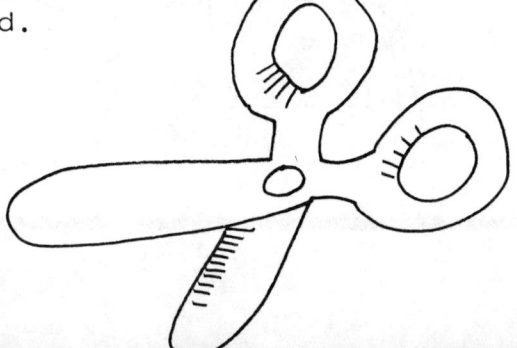

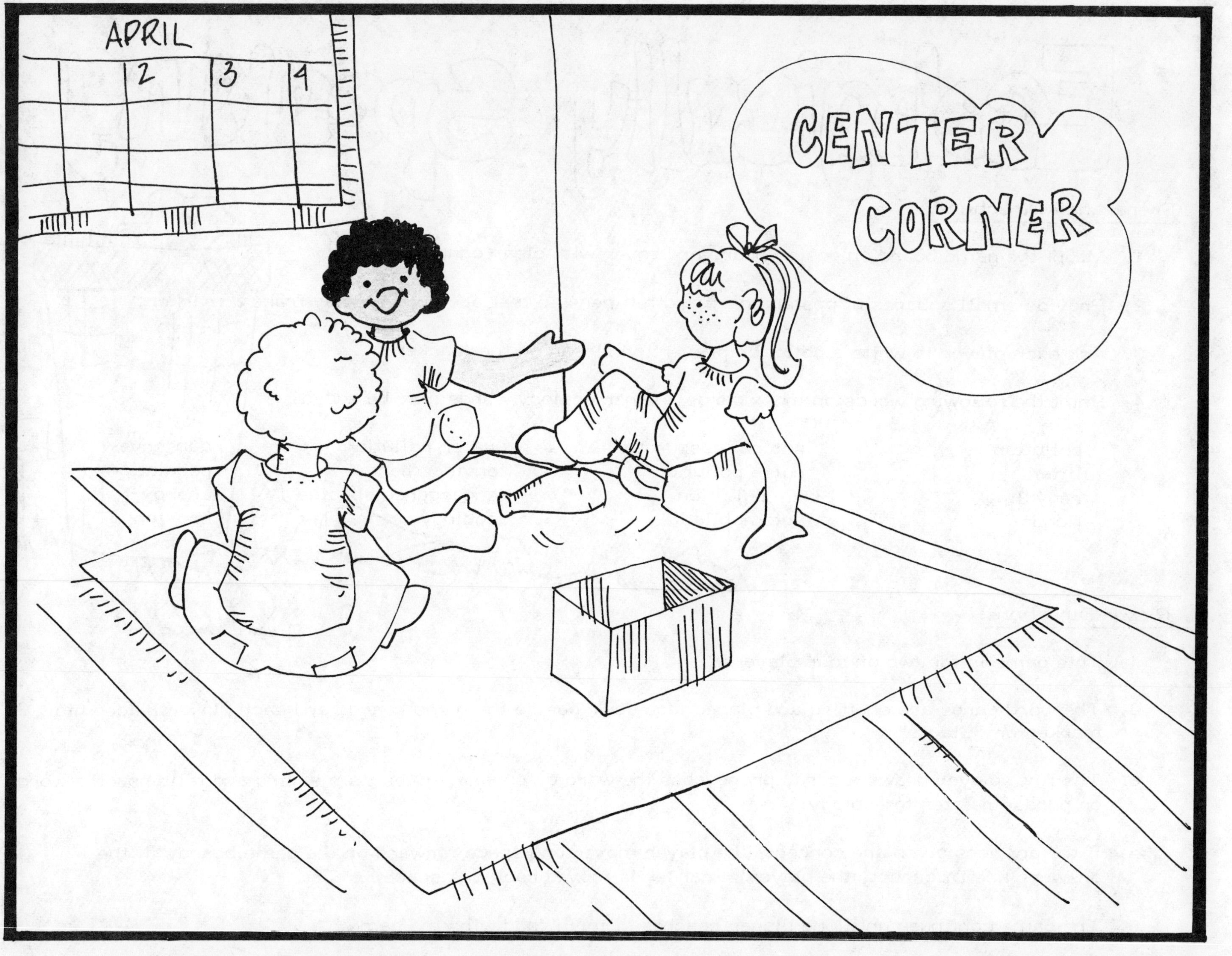
APRIL
2
3
4
CENTER CORNER

Ecologically Speaking

Preparation Directions:

1. Mount the game board on poster board and cover with clear contact paper.

2. Provide small squares of poster board and felt pens so that each player may make a marker.

3. Ask each player to write a pollution prevention slogan on the marker.

4. Print the following words on index cards. Other ecology words may be added.

pollution	natural resources	water pollution	conserve
litter	noise pollution	environment	population
recycling	air pollution	endangered species	energy
floods	automobiles	ecology	erosion

Player Directions:

1. This game is for two or four players.

2. The word cards are shuffled and placed face down beside the game board, and each player places his marker on "Start."

3. The first player draws a card, pronounces the word or phrase, gives its meaning and tells how the word or phrase relates to ecology.

4. If the answers given are correct, the player moves one space forward on the game board. If the answers are incorrect, the player's marker is moved back one space.

5. The game continues until one player reaches "Finish" and wins the game.

START

FINISH

Footprints

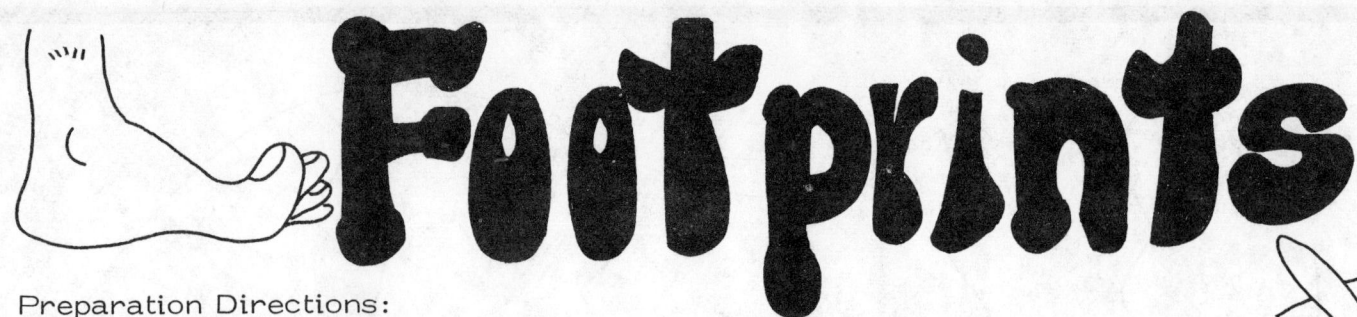

Preparation Directions:

1. Cut out large left and right footprint shapes from brown wrapping paper.

2. Print vocabulary words on the right footprints.

3. Print the definitions of the vocabulary words on the left footprints.

4. Tape the footprints in an interesting pattern on the classroom floor. The vocabulary footprints and definition footprints are not placed together but should be close enough so that students can reach both footprints.

Activity Directions:

1. This activity is for any number of students.

2. The first student places one foot on a vocabulary word and the other foot on its definition.

3. If the two footprints are correctly matched and if the student does not fall down, he or she may then step to the next word and definition, etc.

4. If the vocabulary footprint and the definition footprint do not match, the student must sit down.

5. The activity continues until all the students have an opportunity to travel along the footprints.

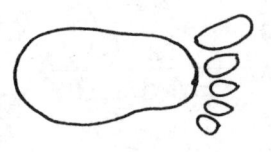

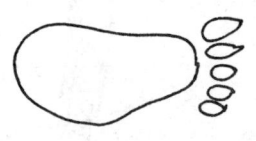

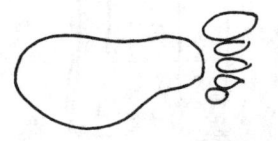

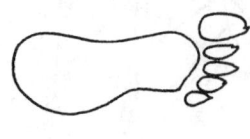

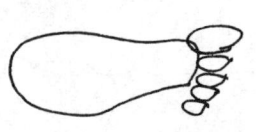

Books We've Read

Fiction Mysteries Biographies

crop whip for a horse

Geography Gamble

Preparation Directions:

1. Mount the game board on poster board and cover it with clear contact paper.

2. Provide a die and markers for each player.

3. Provide a world map or globe as a resource tool.

Player Directions:

1. This game is for two, three or four players.

2. Each player places a marker on "Start."

3. The first player throws the die and moves the correct number of spaces.

4. If the marker lands on "Ocean," the player must name an ocean. If the marker lands on "Sea," the player must name a sea. If the marker lands on "Continent," the player must name a continent. If the marker lands on "Country," the player must name a country, etc.

5. If an incorrect answer is given, the player must go back to the last position of the marker.

6. The game continues until one player reaches "Finish" and wins the game.

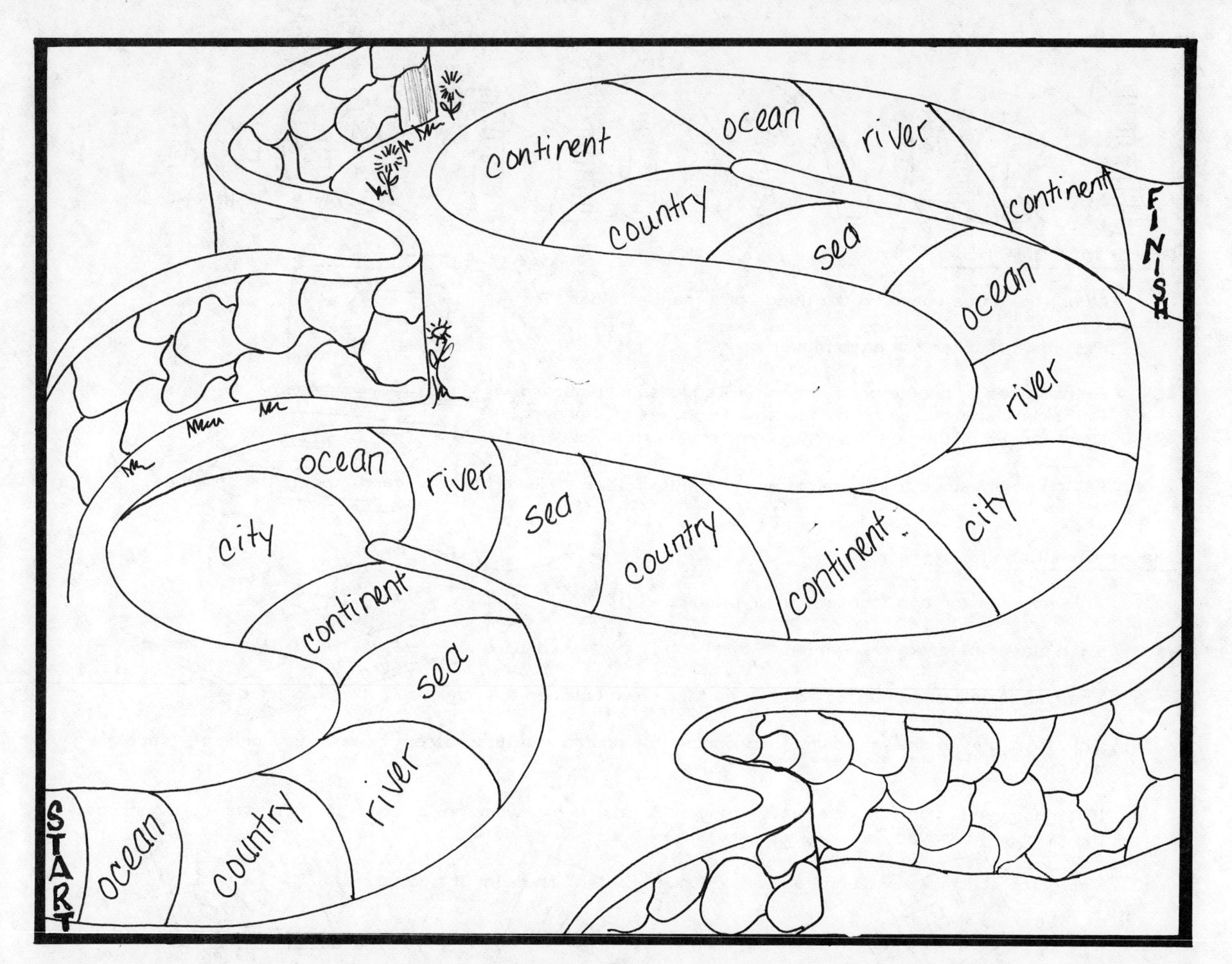

START: ocean → country → river → sea → continent → city → ocean → river → sea → country → continent → city → river → ocean → sea → country → continent → ocean → river → continent **FINISH**

Know Your Nouns

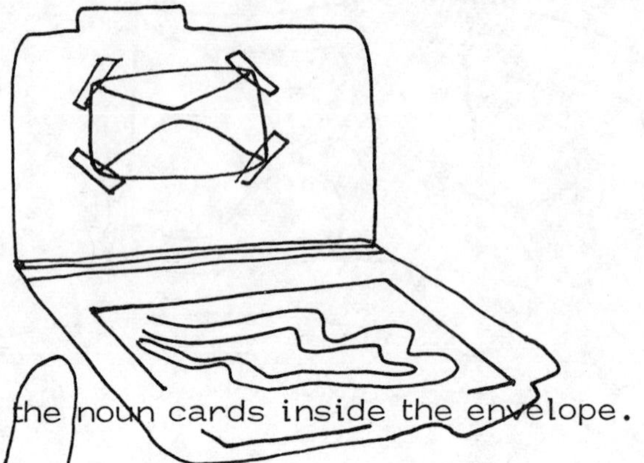

Preparation Directions:

1. Mount the game board on the inside of a manila folder.

2. Provide a marker for each player.

3. Print names of people on twenty small squares of tagboard.
   Print names of places on twenty small squares of tagboard.
   Print names of things on twenty small squares of tagboard.

4. Attach an envelope to the inside of the manila folder. Place the noun cards inside the envelope.

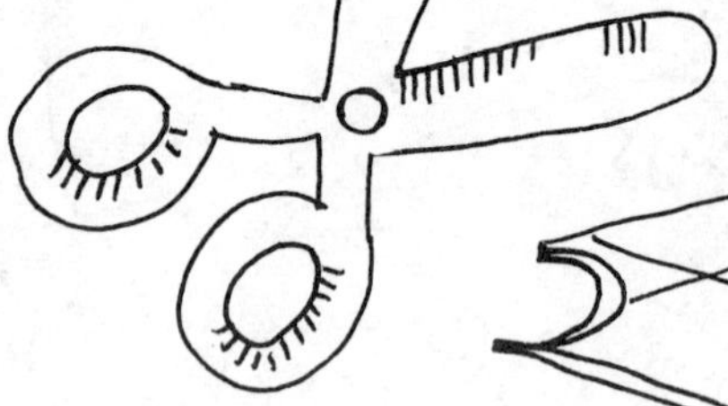

Player Directions:

1. This game is for two, three or four players.

2. Each player places a marker on "Start."

3. The noun cards are shuffled and placed face down between the players.

4. This first player draws a card, pronounces the noun and tells whether the noun is a person, place or thing.

5. If the answer is correct, the player moves the marker forward one space. If the answer is incorrect, the marker is moved back two spaces.

6. The game continues until one player reaches "Finish" and wins the game.

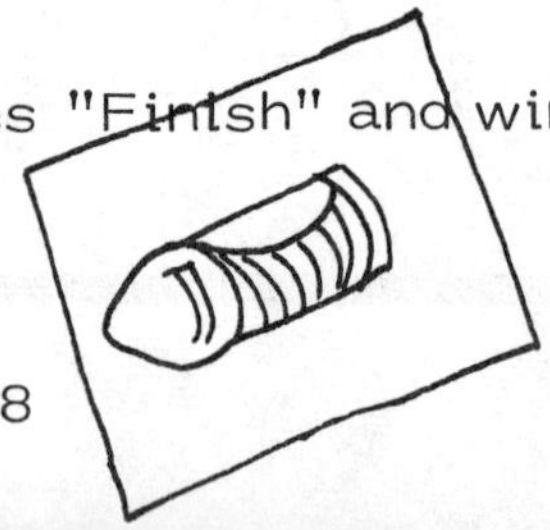

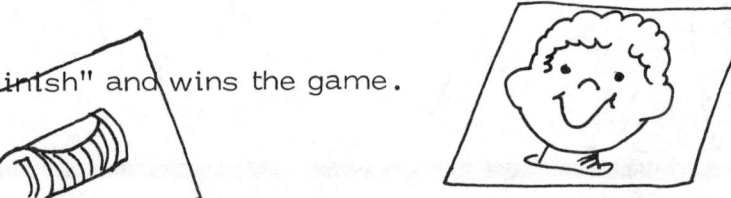

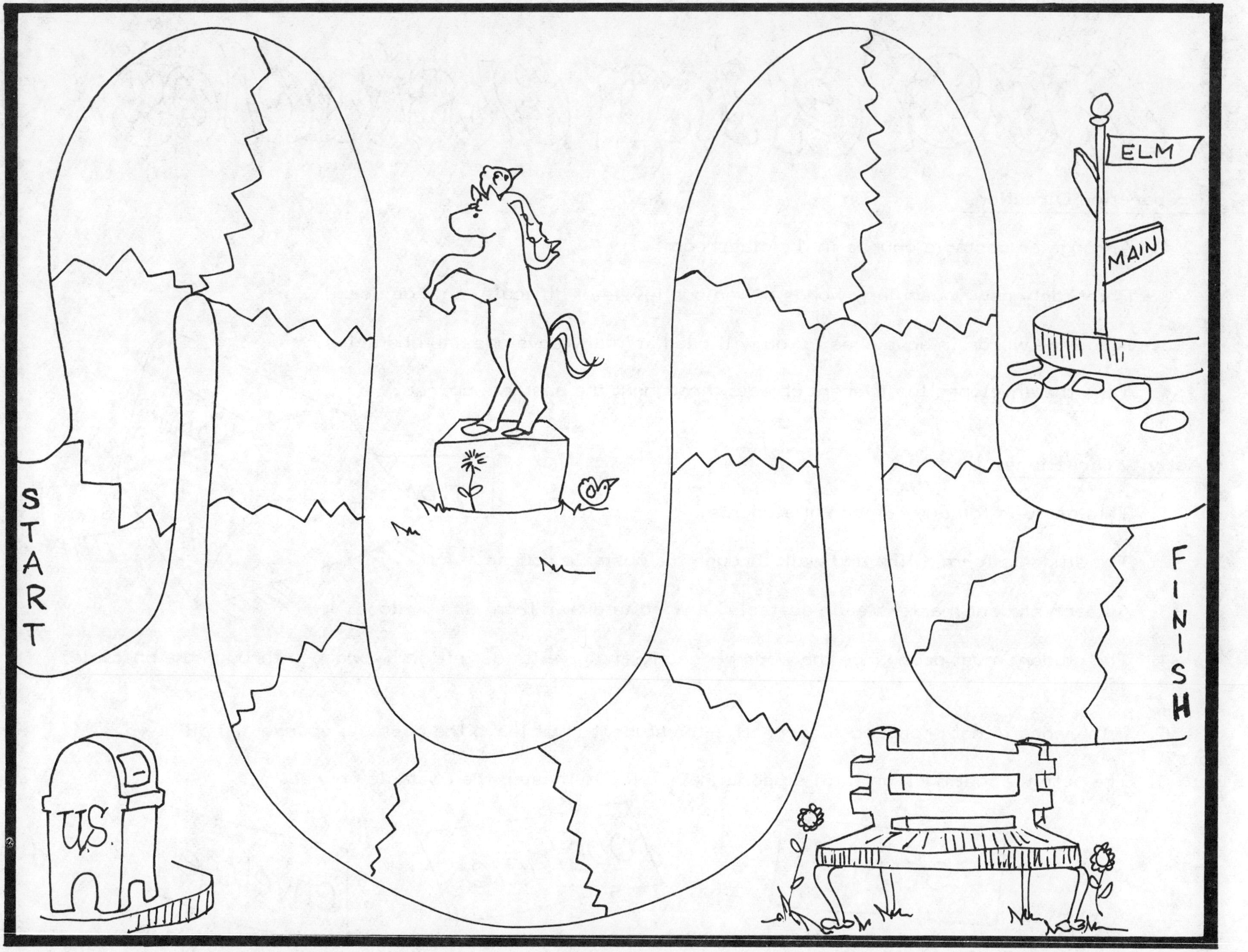
START
FINISH
ELM
MAIN
U.S.

Mastering Obstacles

Preparation Directions:

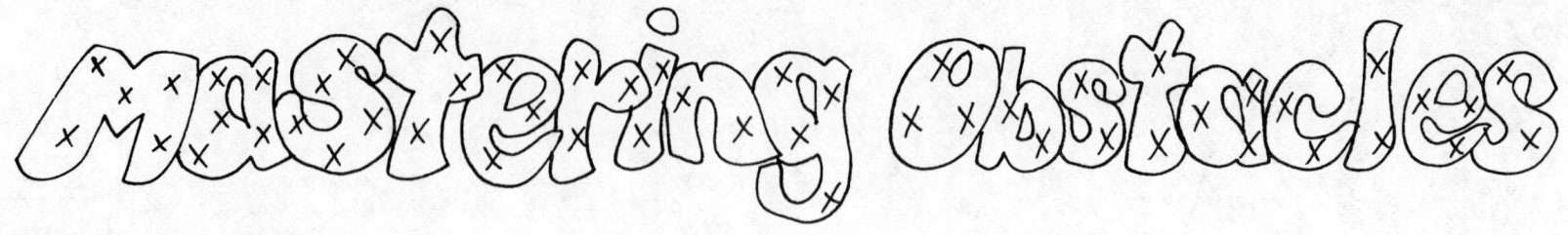

1. Arrange an obstacle course in the classroom.

2. Print forty new vocabulary words of various levels of difficulty on index cards.

3. Place the words in envelopes. You will need as many envelopes as obstacles.

4. Tape the envelopes to different objects throughout the obstacle course.

Activity Directions:

1. This game is for any number of students.

2. The students form a line and walk through the obstacle course.

3. As each student masters each obstacle, a word is drawn from an envelope.

4. The student must pronounce the word correctly and give its definition to proceed through the obstacle course.

5. If the word is not pronounced correctly, the student must leave the obstacle course and sit down.

6. The activity continues until all students have tried to master the obstacle course.

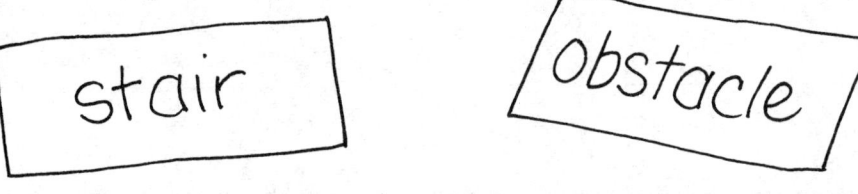

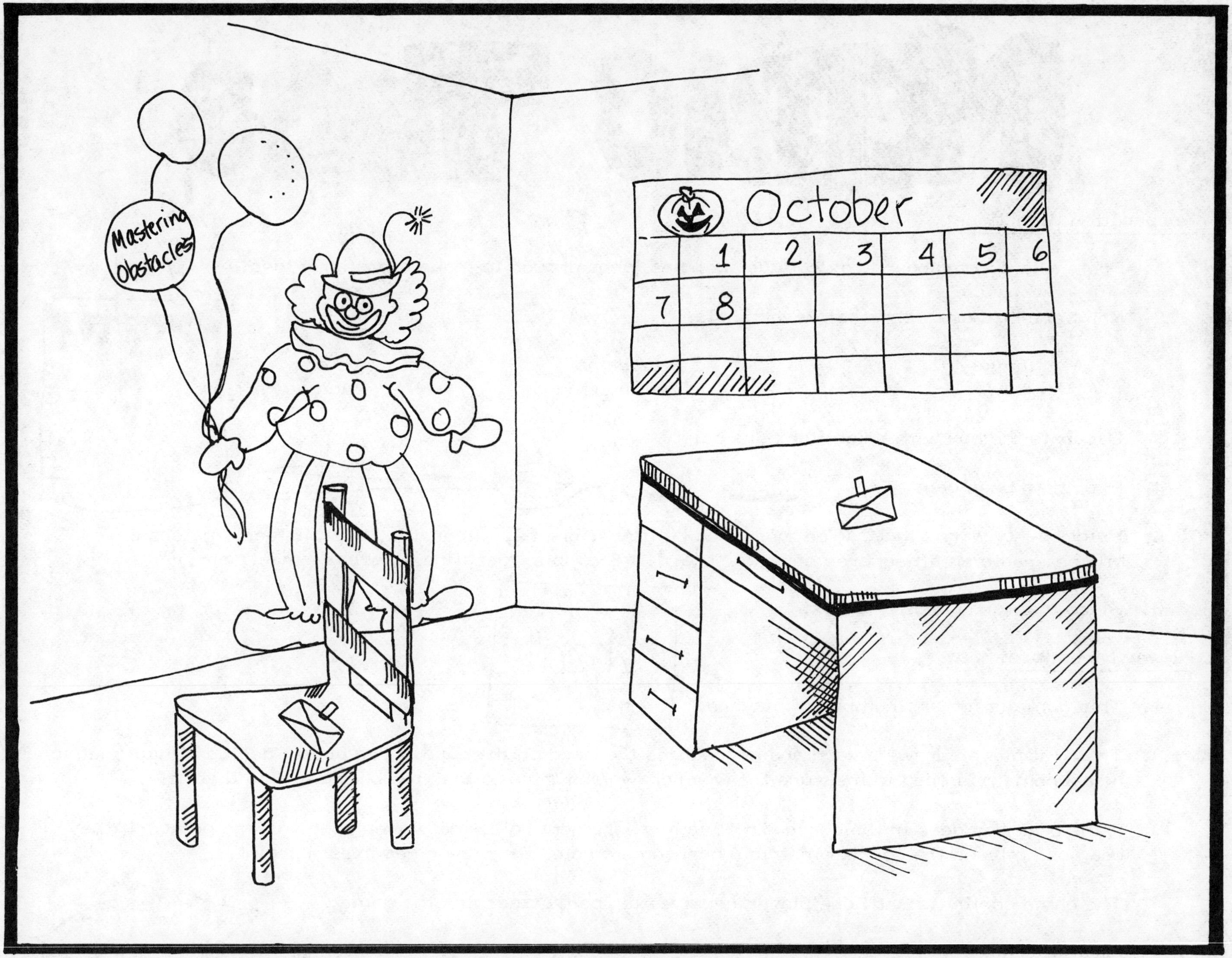
Mastering Obstacles
October
1
2
3
4
5
6
7
8

METRIC TOSS

Preparation Directions:

1. From a large cardboard box cut out six holes large enough to make a bean bag toss.

2. Print one of these words below each hole:

      liters   kilograms   meters
      grams   centimeters   kilometers

3. Decorate the box with bright tempera paint.

4. Provide a bean bag.

5. Print twenty words that can be measured by liters, grams, kilograms, centimeters, meters or kilometers on small squares of poster board. (Example: gasoline – cereal – meat, etc.)

6. Place the word cards in a box.

Player Directions:

1. This game is for any number of players.

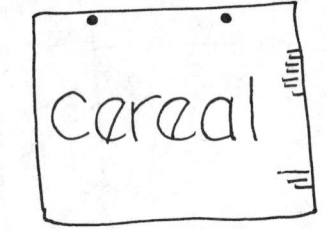

2. The first player draws a card and pronounces the word on the card. The player decides which metric measurement is used to measure the word drawn and tries to toss the bean bag into that hole.

3. If the bean bag goes in the correct metric measurement hole, the player receives one point. If the bean bag misses the correct metric measurement hole, the player receives no point.

4. The game continues until one player receives ten points and wins the game.

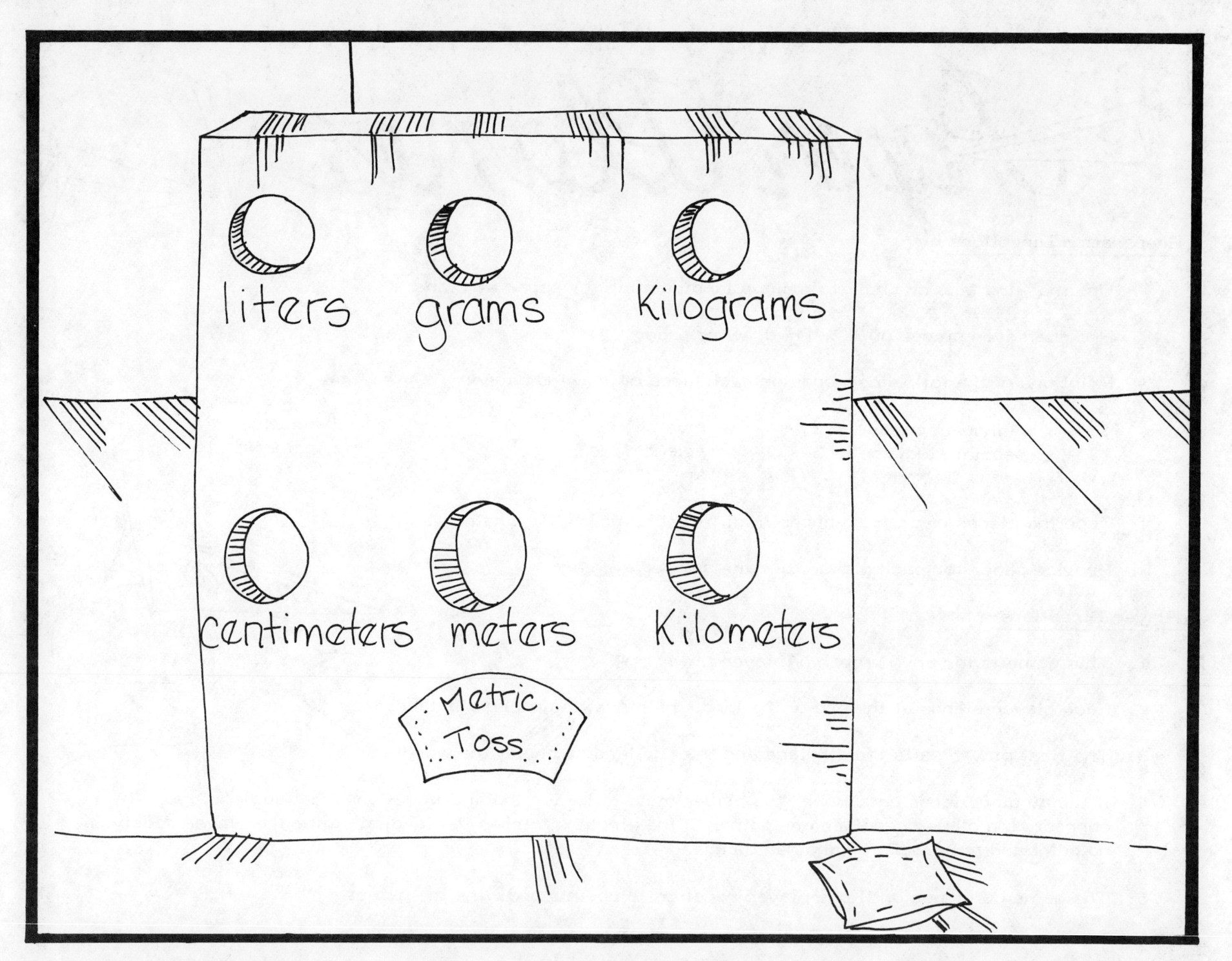

liters   grams   kilograms

centimeters   meters   kilometers

Metric Toss

Paper Planes

Preparation Directions:

1. Use masking tape or chalk to make a landing strip for paper airplanes.

2. Provide seven pieces of 8" x 11" drawing paper.

3. Print one of the following words on each piece of drawing paper:

    language arts   music   mathematics
    social studies   science   physical education
                     art

4. Tape the pieces of drawing paper in different spots on the landing strip.

5. Provide paper for each player to make a paper airplane.

Player Directions:

1. This game is for any number of players.

2. Each player stands at the end of the landing strip with a paper airplane.

3. The first player sails the airplane and tries to land on one of the words.

4. If the airplane lands on a word, the player must tell a vocabulary word from that subject area. If correct, the player receives one point. If the airplane misses the landing strip, the player receives no point and must wait for another turn.

5. The game continues until one player receives ten points and wins the game.

45

Pick a Pair

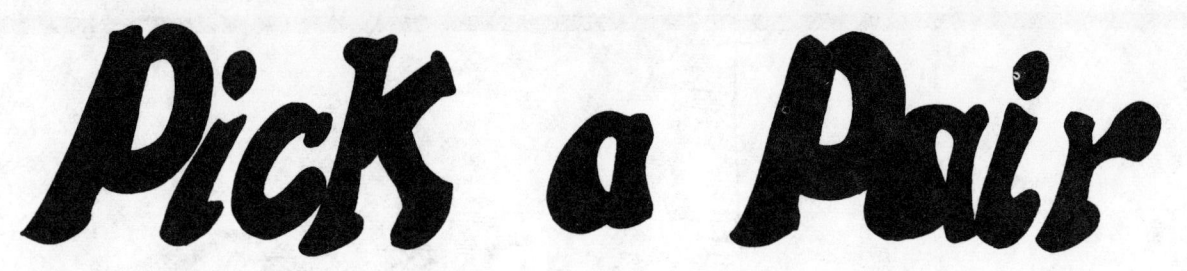

Preparation Directions:

1. Print each new reading, social studies, spelling or science vocabulary word on two different index cards.

2. Cover the back of the index cards with gift-wrapping paper.

Player Directions:

1. This game is for two or four players.

2. The cards are shuffled and each player is given six cards.

3. The remaining cards are placed face down between the players.

4. If a player has two vocabulary words that are the same, they form a "book" and are placed on the table.

5. The first player asks another player for a card with a certain vocabulary word on it. (Example: "Do you have the word _____?") The player must pronounce the vocabulary word correctly.

6. If the second player has that card, he or she must give it to the first player. Then the first player is allowed another turn.

7. If the second player does not have the vocabulary card asked for, the first player draws a card from the stack and the next player takes a turn.

8. The game continues until all the vocabulary cards have been called and formed into "books."

9. The player who has the most "books" wins the game.

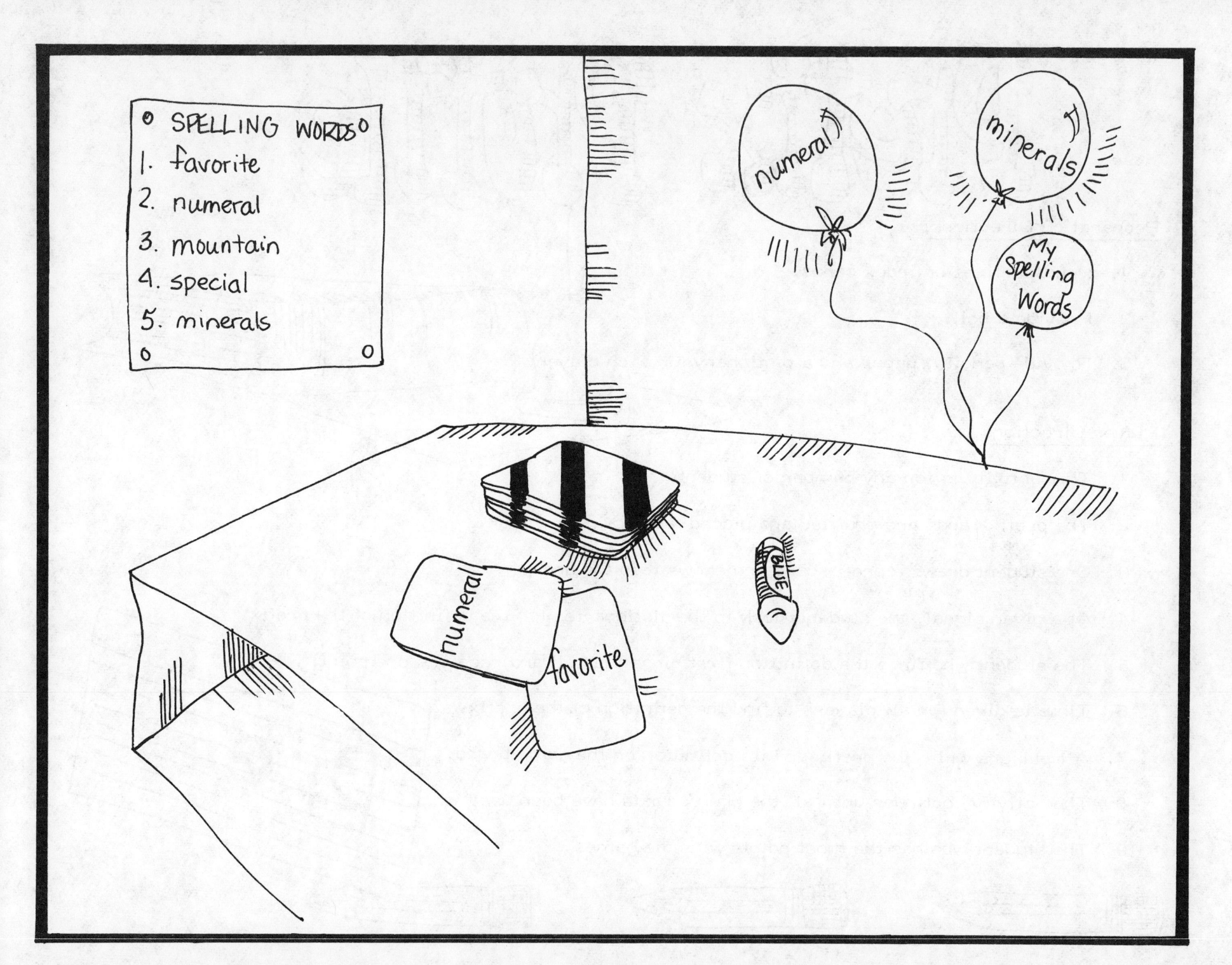

SPELLING WORDS
1. favorite
2. numeral
3. mountain
4. special
5. minerals

Prefix Profile

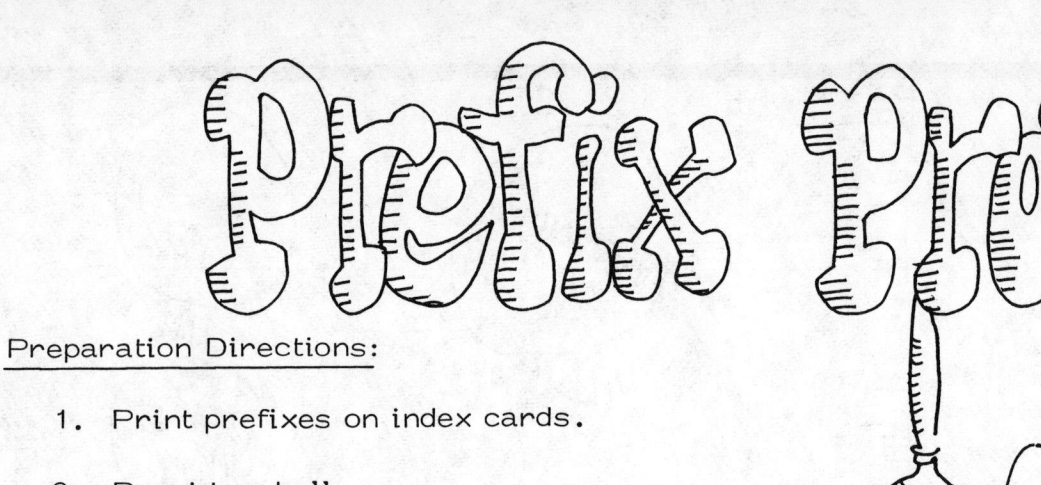

Preparation Directions:

1. Print prefixes on index cards.

2. Provide a bell.

3. Provide pencils, paper and a dictionary for each player.

Player Directions:

1. This activity is for any number of students.

2. The prefix cards are shuffled and placed face down on a desk.

3. One student draws a prefix card and shows it to the group.

4. At a given signal, the students look in the dictionaries for the definition of the prefix.

5. The student who finds the definition first rings the bell and receives one point.

6. Time is given for all players to find the definition of the prefix.

7. All players write the prefix and its definition on the game board.

8. The activity continues until all the prefix cards have been used.

9. The student who has the most points wins the game.

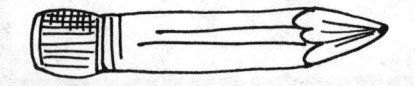

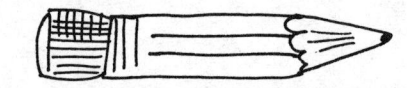

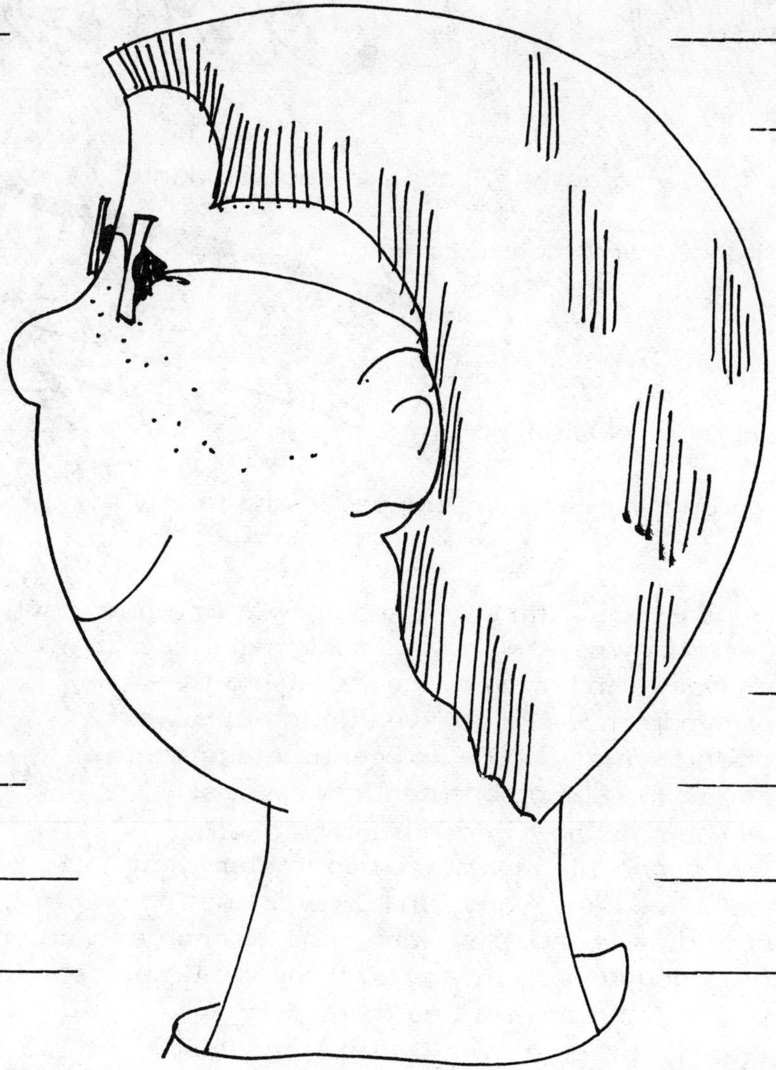

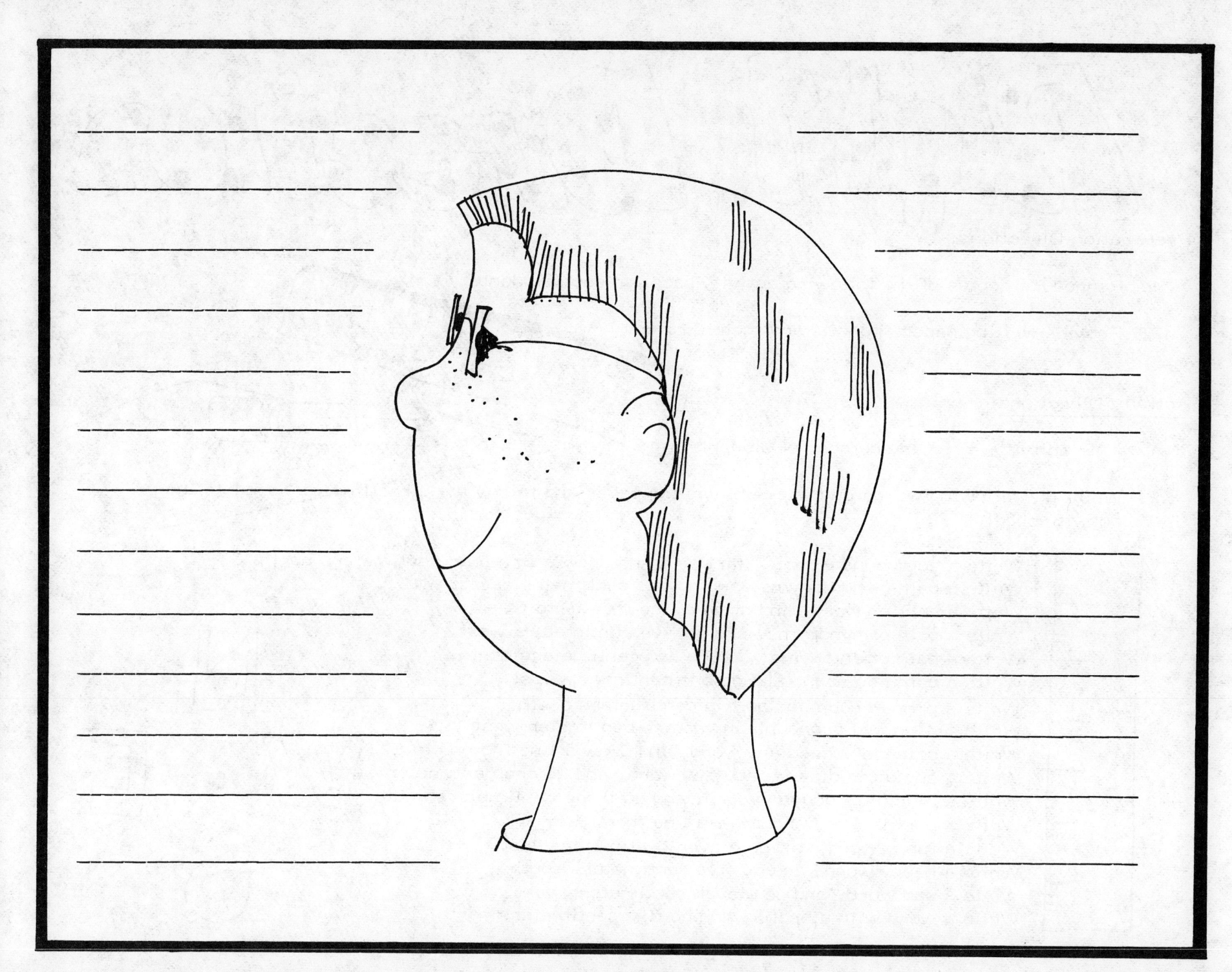

Right Direction

Preparation Directions:

1. Reproduce copies of the following activity page for each student.

2. Provide writing paper, pencils and metric rulers.

Activity Directions:

1. This activity is for any number of students.

2. Write the following words on a piece of writing paper and follow the directions to complete the activity sheet.

Write a compound word. Start at A and draw a line four centimeters north.
Write a pair of homonyms, and go one centimeter east.
Write an action word, and draw a line from B to C.
Write a pair of synonyms, and go five centimeters west.
Write a pair of antonyms, and go two centimeters north.
Write a common noun, and go one centimeter west.
Write a proper noun and go two centimeters south.
Write a personal pronoun, and go one centimeter west.
Write a science vocabulary word, and draw a line from D to E.
Write a social studies vocabulary word, and go one centimeter east.
Write a music vocabulary word, and go three centimeters south.
Write a contraction, and draw a line from F to G.
Write a funny word, and go eleven centimeters east.
Write a happy word, and go five centimeters south.
Write a sad word, and go eleven centimeters west.
Write a word with a prefix, and go five centimeters north.

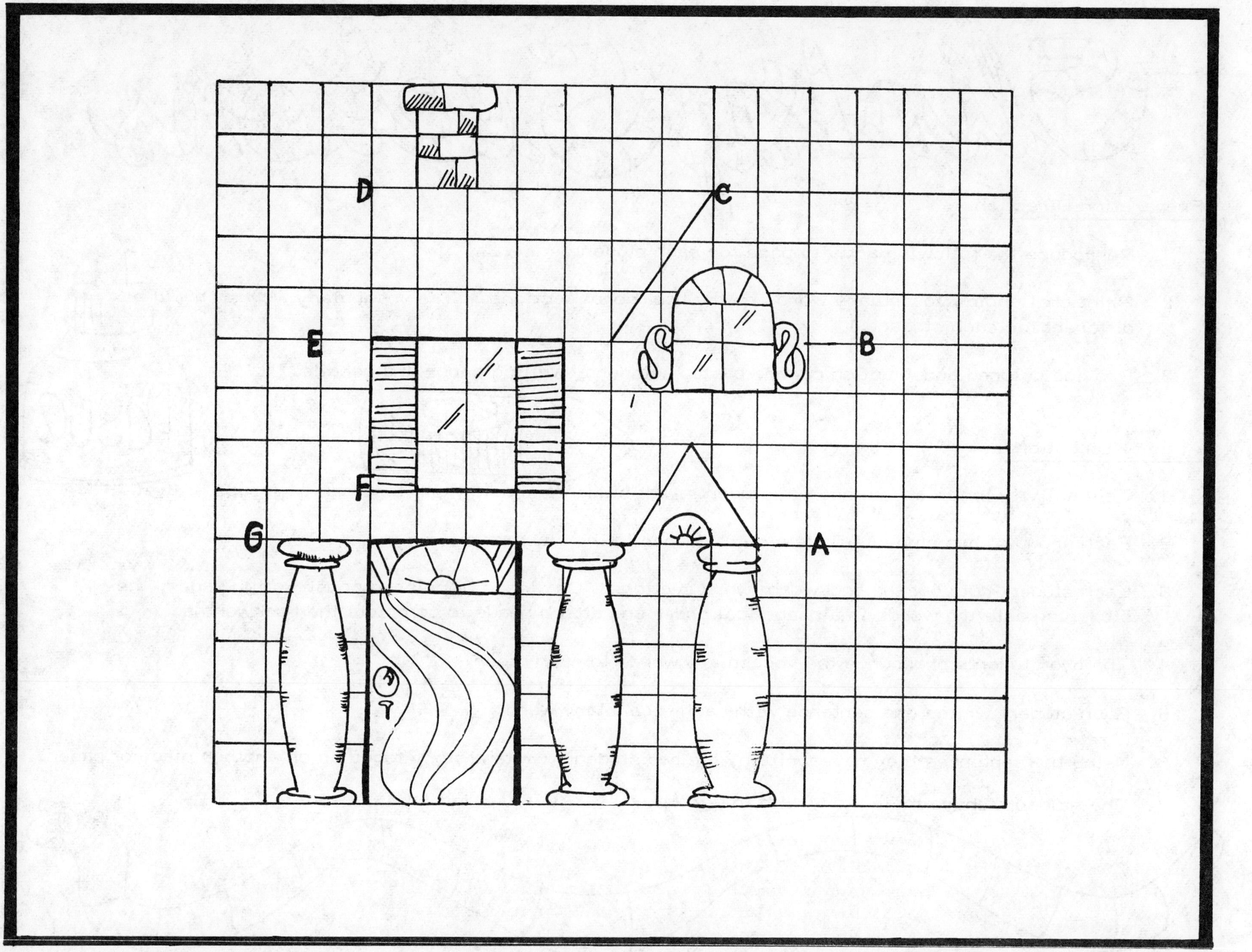
D
C
E
B
F
G
A

Slinky Sections

Preparation Directions:

1. Reproduce the following activity page for each student.

2. Print challenging vocabulary words on the bookworm sections. (The vocabulary words should be different for each student.)

3. Provide colored construction paper, paste, scissors, writing paper and pencils.

Activity Directions:

1. This activity is for any number of students, but students should work together in groups of two.

2. Each group of two students finds a quiet corner in the classroom.

3. Each student cuts out the bookworm word sections. On pieces of colored construction paper, the students paste the words in alphabetical order and attach heads to complete the bookworms.

4. The two students pronounce the vocabulary words to each other.

5. Each student writes one sentence with each vocabulary word.

6. Using the sentences they have written, the two students write a story together on another piece of paper.

7. The students share their story with the group.

53

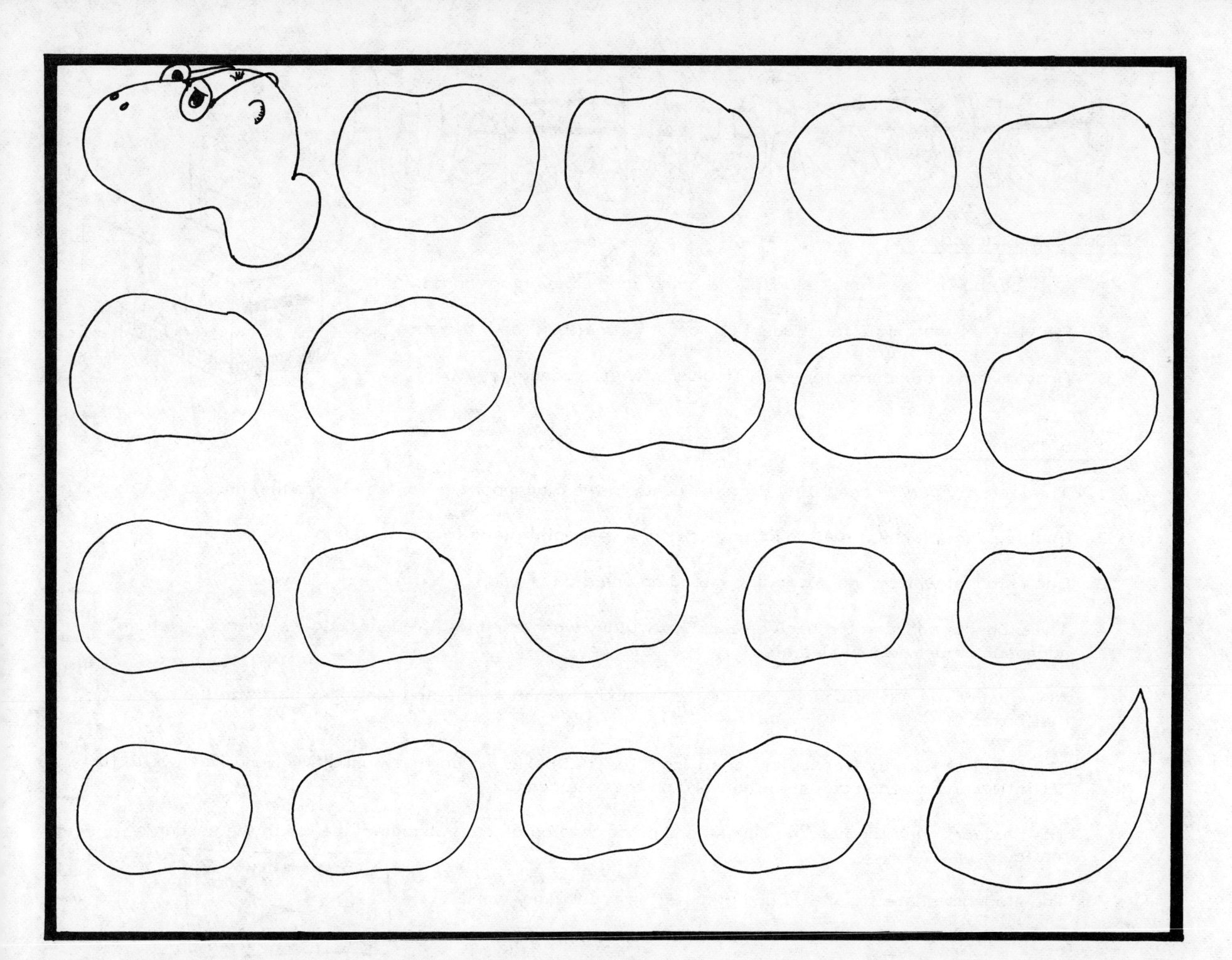

Special Mail

Preparation Directions:

1. Collect shoe boxes or ask students to bring shoe boxes from home.

2. Provide art materials for students to create a mailbox from the shoe box.

3. Provide ten index cards for each student to write vocabulary words.

Activity Directions:

1. This activity can be used for all the students in the classroom or for small reading groups.

2. Each student places a mailbox on a desk or at a special place in the classroom.

3. Each student writes one vocabulary word on one side of each of the ten index cards.

4. The students address the back of each vocabulary word card to different fellow students. Return addresses must be included also!

5. At a given time, the students deliver the vocabulary mail by placing the index cards in the correct mailboxes.

6. The students take the vocabulary mail from the mailboxes, read the vocabulary word, and write its definition and a sentence using the word on the index card.

7. The students read the return address and place the completed vocabulary cards in the sender's mailbox.

8. The students share the cards and discuss the vocabulary words.

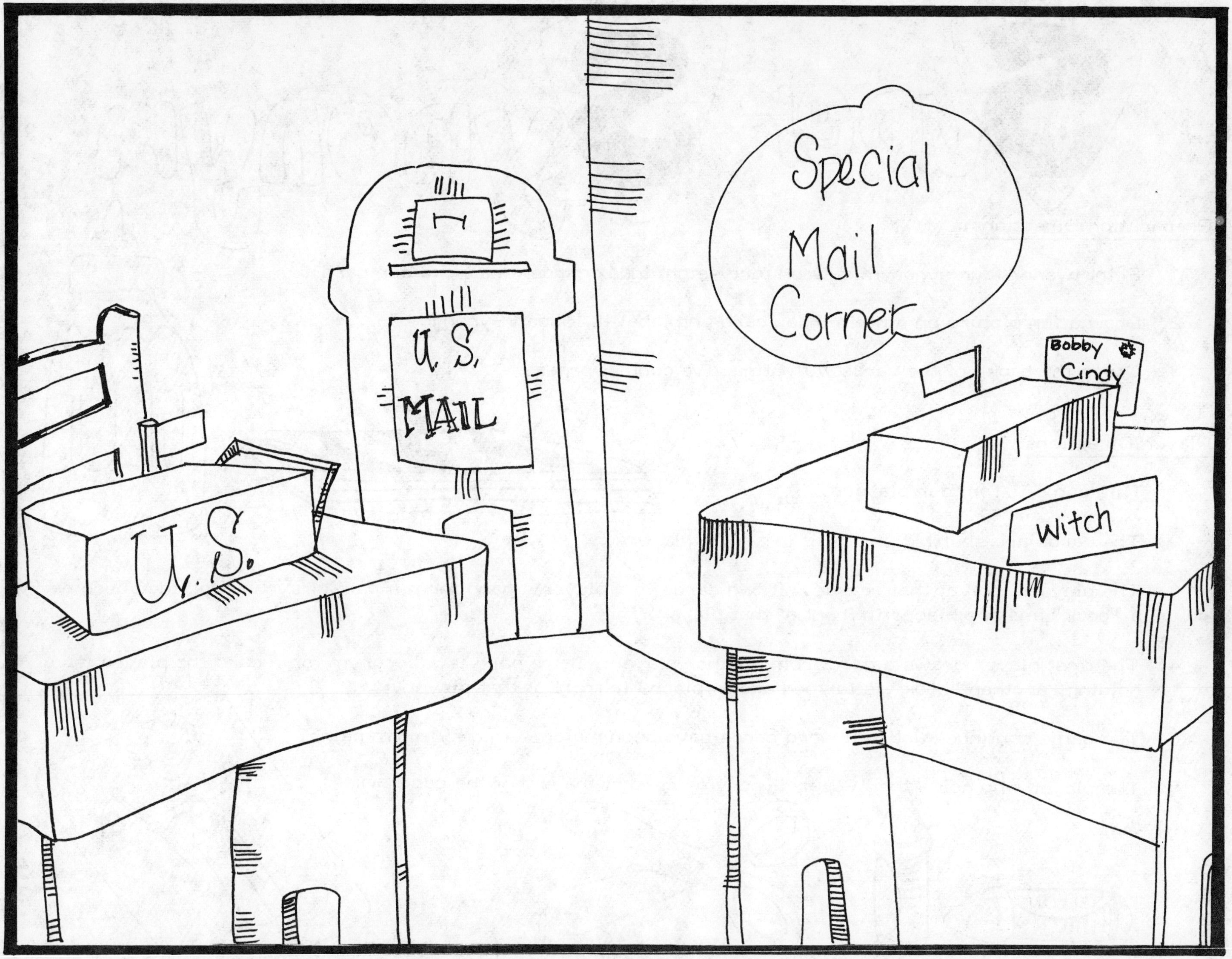
Special
Mail
Corner
U.S.
MAIL
U.S.
Bobby
Cindy
witch

Super Synonym

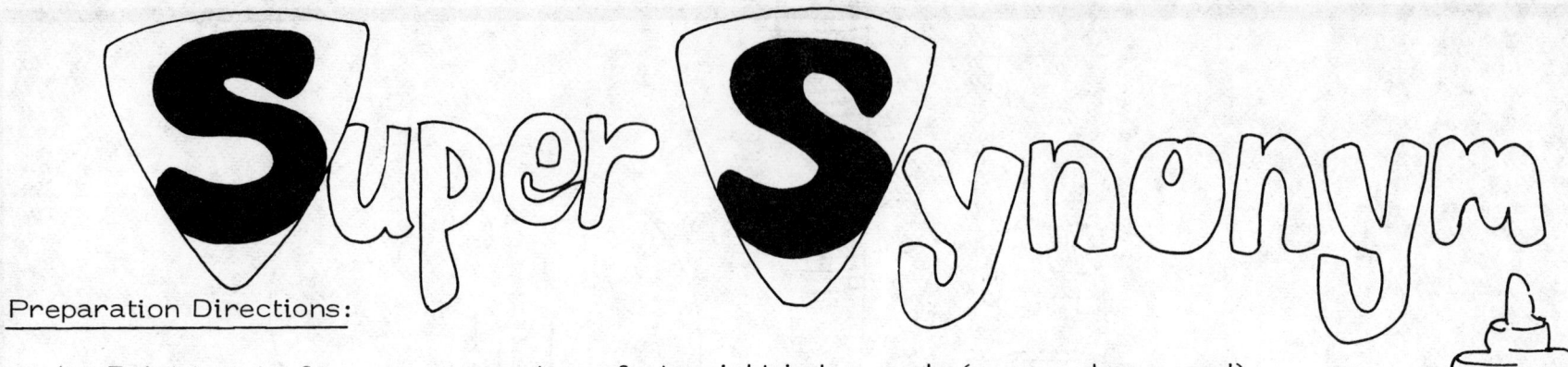

Preparation Directions:

1. Print twenty-four synonym sets on forty-eight index cards (one word per card).

2. Draw a fun picture on a plain index card and label it "Super Synonym."

3. Cover the backs of the cards with attractive contact paper.

Player Directions:

1. This game is for four players.

2. The cards are shuffled and dealt to all the players.

3. The players look at their cards. If two cards in a player's hand form a pair of synonyms, they become a "book" and are placed in front of that player.

4. The first player draws a card from another player. If the card is a synonym for a card the player is holding, another "book" is formed and is placed in front of that player.

5. The game continues until all word cards have been matched into synonym pairs.

6. The player who holds the "Super Synonym" card at the end of the game wins.

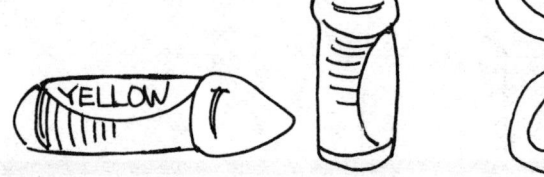

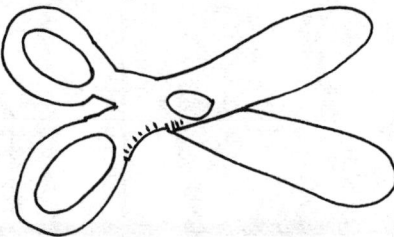

sick

mad angry

S

RED YELLOW

Take a Nibble

Preparation Directions:

1. Provide yellow construction paper for each player to make a shape resembling a piece of cheese.

2. Provide a hole punch.

3. Use gray construction paper and draw forty shapes to resemble mice.

4. Print a vocabulary word on each mouse.

Player Directions:

1. This game is for two, three or four players.

2. Each player has a piece of cheese.

3. Shuffle the mice vocabulary cards and place them on a desk.

4. The first player draws a mouse vocabulary card and pronounces the word.

5. If the word is pronounced correctly, the player punches one hole in the piece of cheese.

6. The game continues until all mice have been drawn and the words pronounced correctly. The player whose cheese has the most holes punched in it wins the game.

hilarious

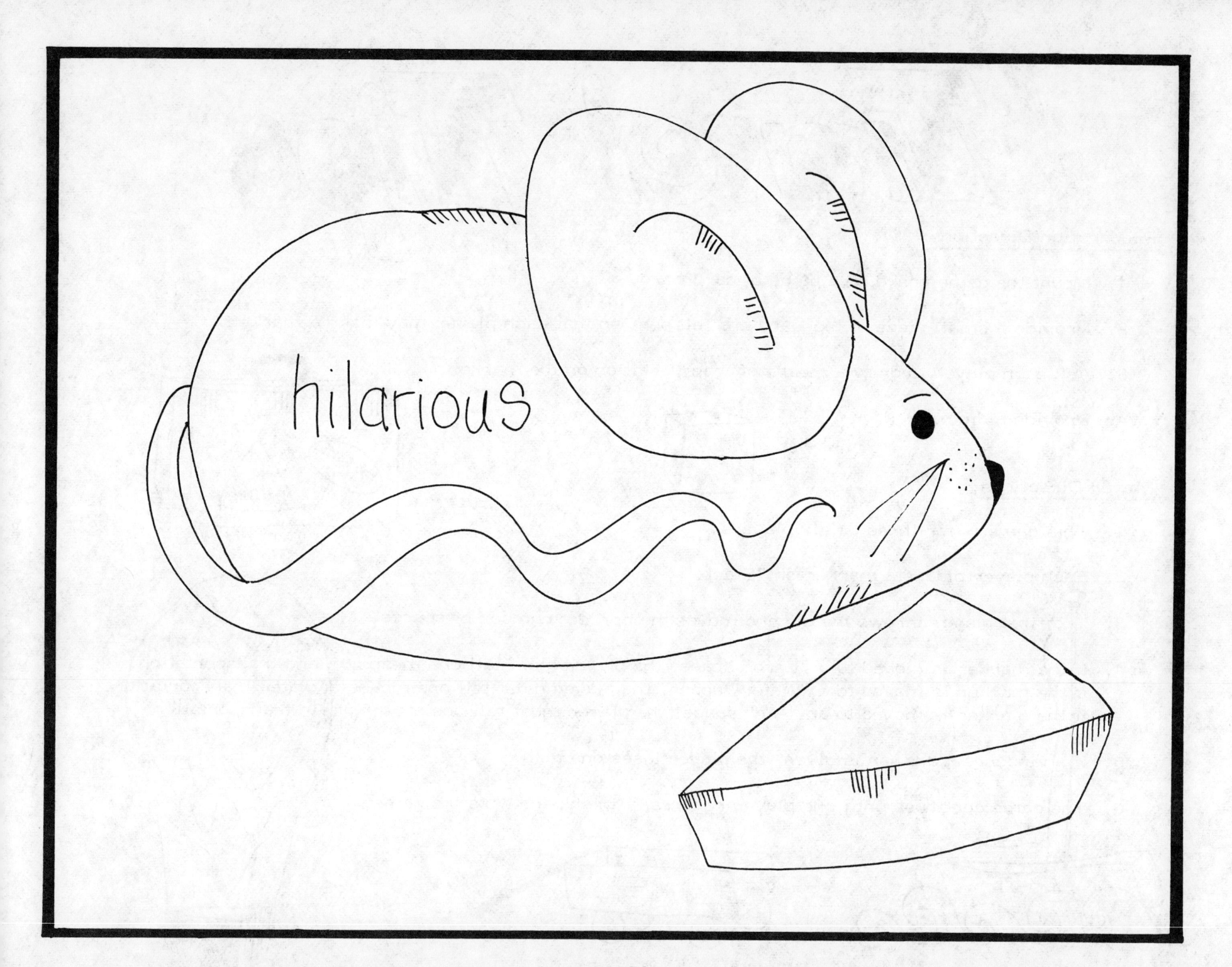

Travel Tips

Preparation Directions:

1. Mount the game board on a piece of cardboard.

2. Provide a small piece of tagboard and felt pens so that each player may make a marker.

3. Ask each player to draw a means of transportation on the marker.

4. Provide a die.

Player Directions:

1. This game is for three or six players.

2. Each player places a marker on "Start."

3. The first player throws the die and moves the correct number of spaces.

4. If the marker is moved to a "Land" space, the player must tell one means of land transportation. If the marker is moved to a "Water" space, the player must tell one means of water transportation. If the marker is moved to an "Air" space, the player must tell one means of air transportation.

5. If an incorrect answer is given, the player loses one turn.

6. The game continues until one player reaches "Finish" and wins the game.

Finish

Water | Land | Air | Water | Land | Air

Water

Air

Land

Air | Water | Air | Land | Water

Land

Start

61

Word Walk

Preparation Directions:

1. Use masking tape or chalk to make a Word Walk on the classroom floor (see example on the following page).

2. Print on index cards new vocabulary words that have been presented in language arts, mathematics, science or social studies. You will need as many numbers on the Word Walk as there are vocabulary words.

3. Write a number on each vocabulary card. The numbers must correspond to the numbers on the Word Walk.

4. Place the word cards in a box.

5. Provide a record player and a record.

Activity Directions:

1. This activity is for any number of students.

2. The students stand on any number on the Word Walk. The teacher or one student operates the record player and starts the music.

3. As long as the music is playing, the students must walk around the Word Walk. When the operator stops the music, the students must stop at the same time on the number closest to them.

4. The operator draws a word card and tells the number on the card. The student standing on that number on the Word Walk must take the card and pronounce the vocabulary word.

5. If the vocabulary word is not pronounced correctly, the student must sit down. The game continues until only one student is left standing on the Word Walk. That student wins the game.

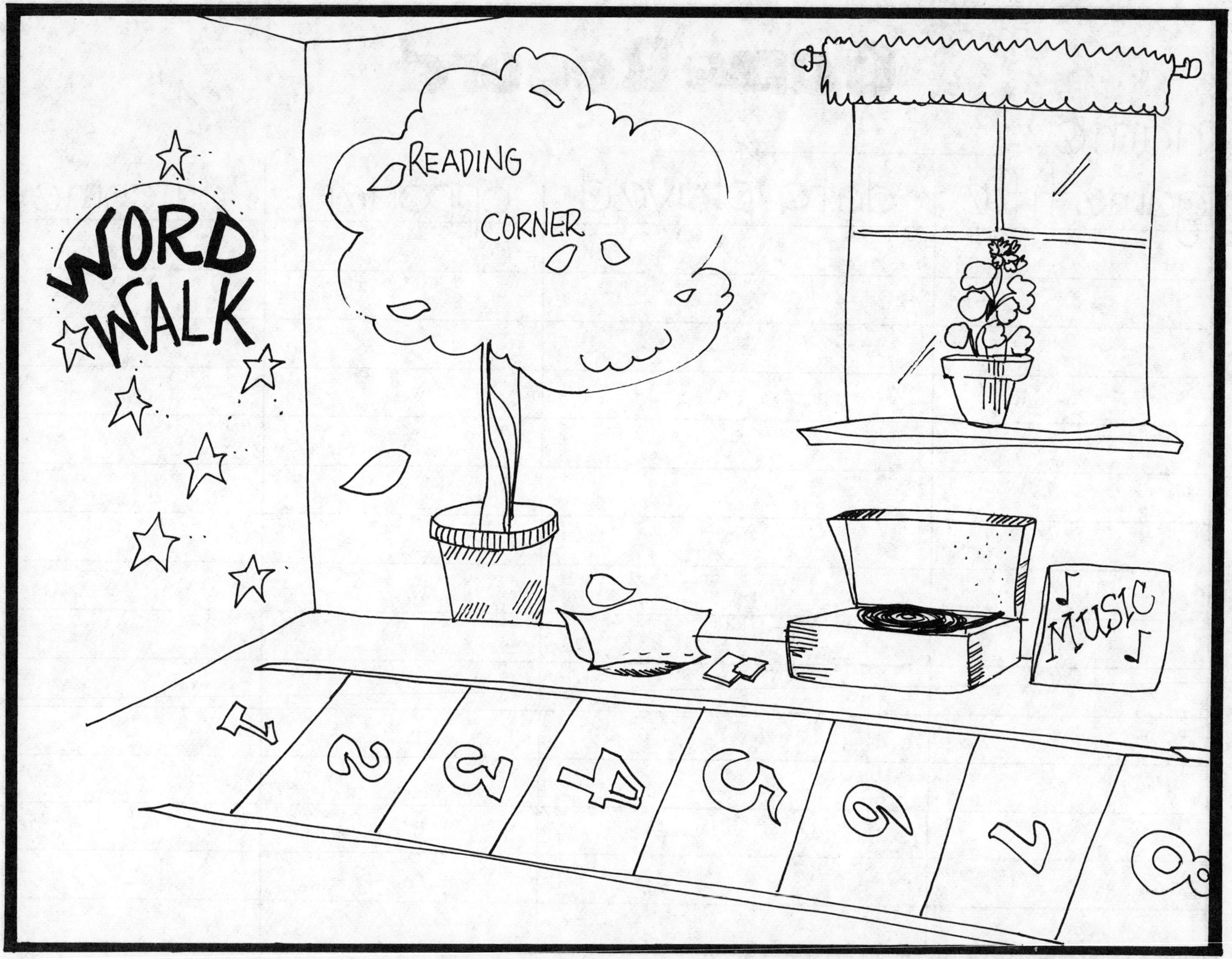
WORD WALK
READING CORNER
MUSIC
1
2
3
4
5
6
7
8

Game Record

name: _____

game title	date played	opponent	outcome

SKILLS DEVELOPMENT ACTIVITIES

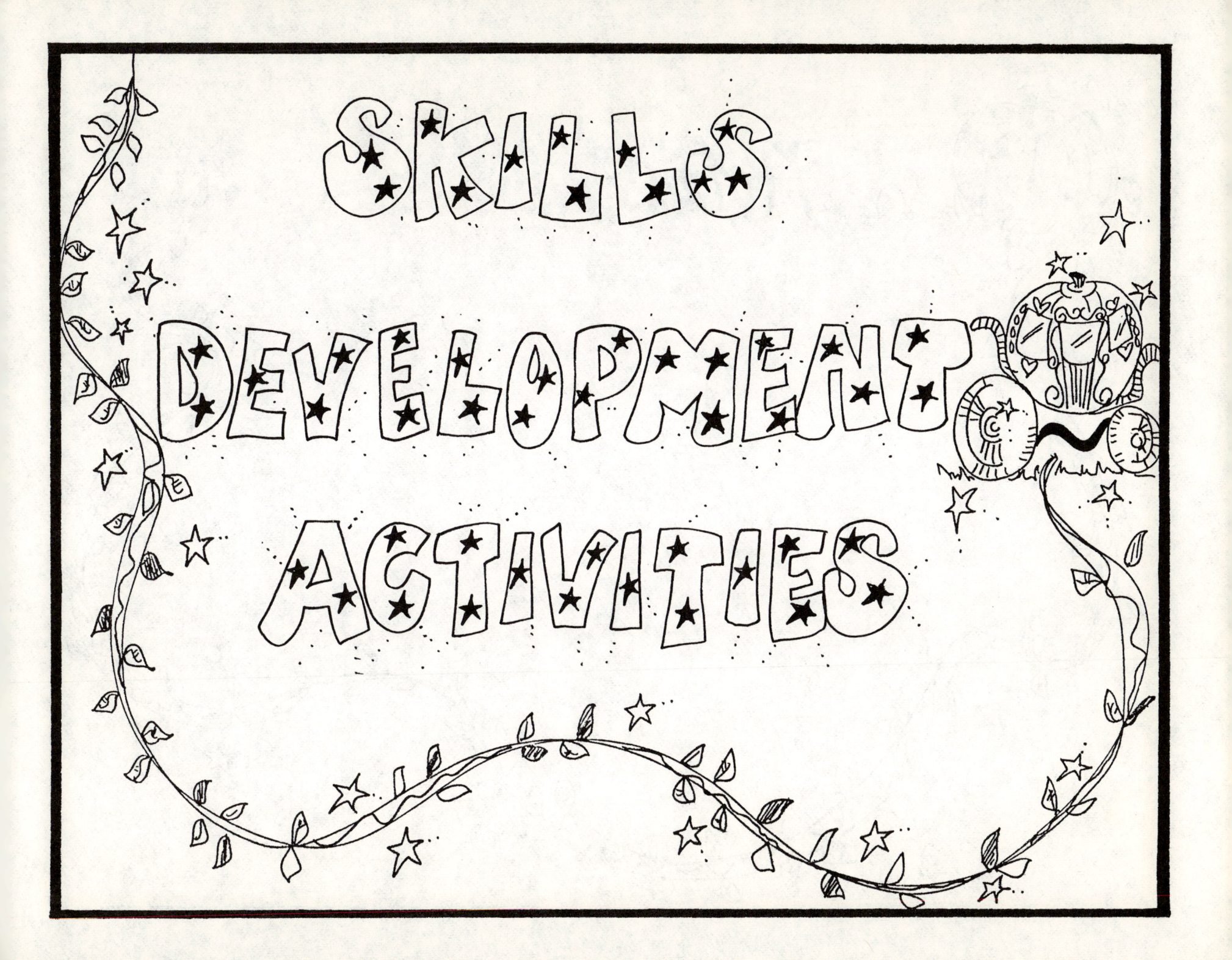

Notes

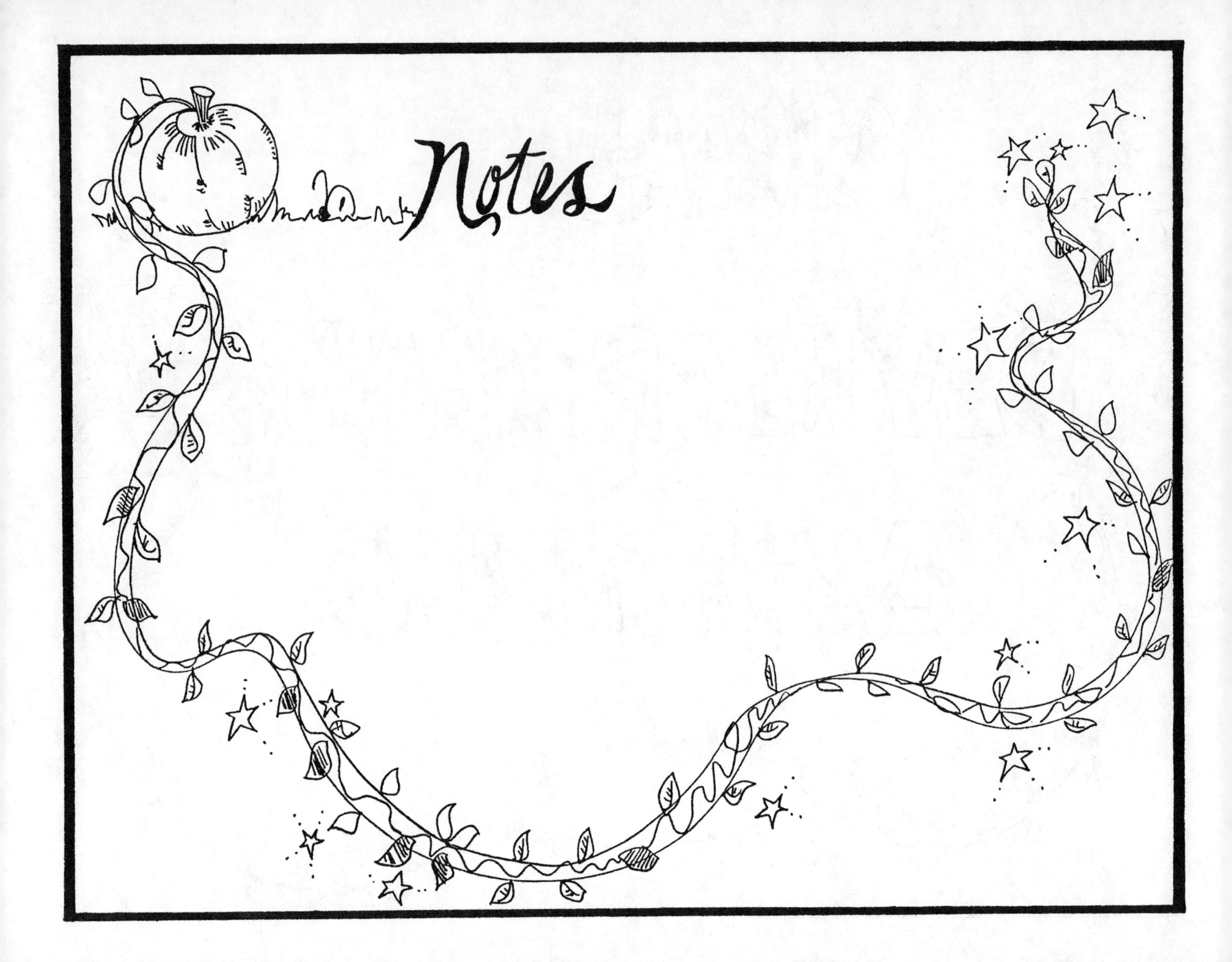

ALPHABET JUNCTION

Preparation Directions:

1. Reproduce copies of the Alphabet Junction activity sheets on the following pages.

2. Provide dictionaries, pencils, writing paper, white drawing paper, scissors and crayons.

3. Print the student directions on a chart or task card if the activity is to be used in a learning center or other independent setting. If used as a group activity or an individually guided student project, the directions may be given orally.

Student Directions:

1. Read the directions on each of the Alphabet Junction activity sheets very carefully before you begin.

2. Use a dictionary for help if you need it.

3. Discuss your completed work with the teacher.

Alphabet Junction is the next stop! As you leave the train, write a word beginning with each letter of the alphabet on strips of white drawing paper. Cut along the dotted line and place the words in the train. Enjoy your visit at Alphabet Junction by coloring the train and adding background scenery.

Write as many words as possible in each of the following categories.
(Example: Action Words – run, jump, skip, leap, sprint, hop, etc.)

Aviation Words _____

Beautiful Words _____

Cartoon Words _____

Christmas Words _____

Dignified Words _____

Emotional Words _____

Funny Words _____

Geography Words _____

Historical Words _____

Inventive Words _____

Job Words _____

Kinsfolk Words _____

Library Words _____

Ocean Words

Royal Words

Metric Words _____

Noisy Words _____

Ocean Words _____

Pollution Words _____

Quiet Words _____

Royal Words _____

Social Words _____

Teacher Words _____

Umpire Words _____

Vogue Words _____

Weather Words _____

Youthful Words _____

Zoo Words _____

Zoo Words

Weather Words

Contraction Comedian

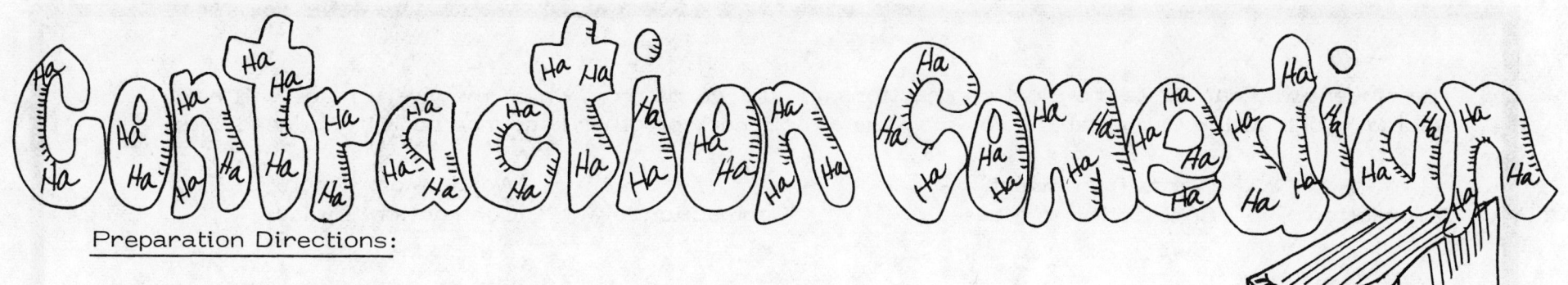

Preparation Directions:

1. Reproduce copies of the Contraction Comedian activity sheets on the following pages.

2. Provide dictionaries, pencils and writing paper.

3. Print the student directions on a chart or task card if the activity is to be used in a learning center or other independent setting. If used as a group activity or an individually guided student project, the directions may be given orally.

4. Discuss and review previous work with contractions.

5. Ask students to assist in listing commonly used contractions on a chart or on the chalkboard.

Student Directions:

1. Read the directions on each of the Contraction Comedian activity sheets very carefully before you begin. Use your imagination and pretend that you actually are a comedian. Make sure your work is correct, but remember that humor is very important in these activities.

2. Use your dictionary or other resource books for help if you need it.

3. Discuss your completed work with the teacher.

The student who can write the most contractions and the words from which they were made will be elected "Contraction Comedian." You may use a dictionary or other resource book if you need help.

Contraction	Words from which Contraction is Made	Contraction	Words from which Contraction is Made
_____	_____	_____	_____
_____	_____	_____	_____
_____	_____	_____	_____
_____	_____	_____	_____
_____	_____	_____	_____
_____	_____	_____	_____
_____	_____	_____	_____
_____	_____	_____	_____

Congratulations! You won the title of "Contraction Comedian." You will be asked to perform often, so many scripts are needed for your acts. Write a joke, a riddle and a song for the grand opening of your show. Include contractions in the joke, riddle and song.

Joke

Song

Riddle

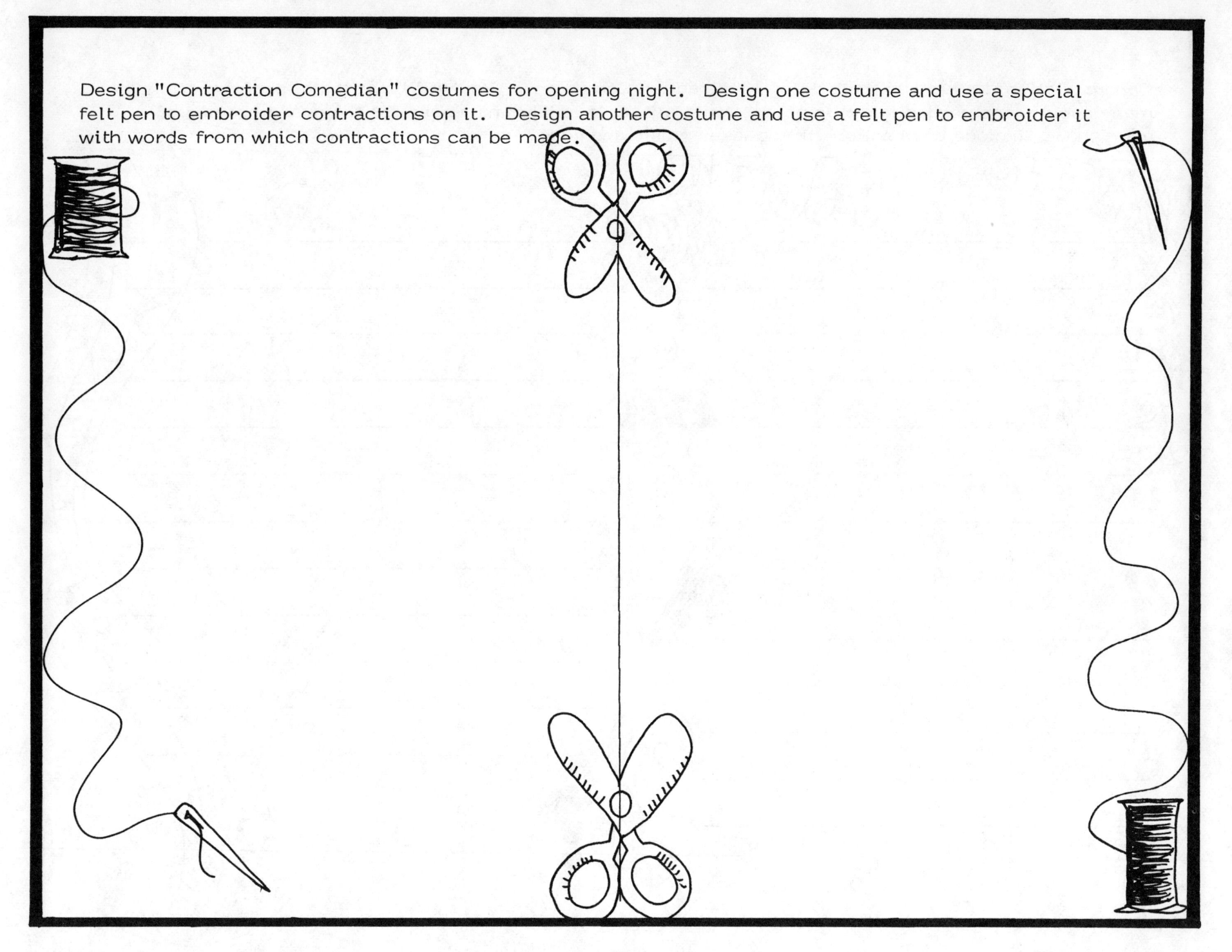

Design "Contraction Comedian" costumes for opening night. Design one costume and use a special felt pen to embroider contractions on it. Design another costume and use a felt pen to embroider it with words from which contractions can be made.

Fun House

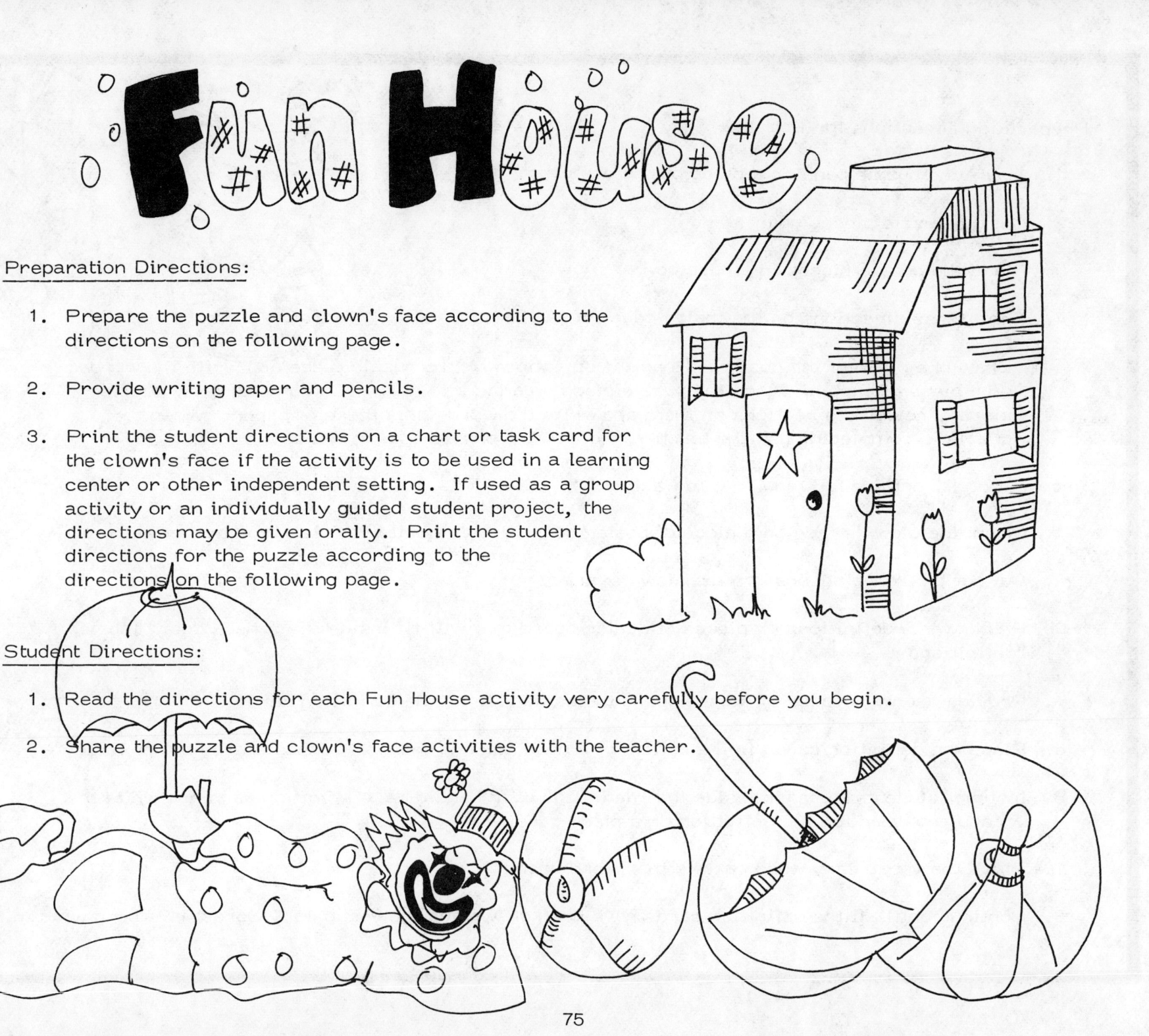

Preparation Directions:

1. Prepare the puzzle and clown's face according to the directions on the following page.

2. Provide writing paper and pencils.

3. Print the student directions on a chart or task card for the clown's face if the activity is to be used in a learning center or other independent setting. If used as a group activity or an individually guided student project, the directions may be given orally. Print the student directions for the puzzle according to the directions on the following page.

Student Directions:

1. Read the directions for each Fun House activity very carefully before you begin.

2. Share the puzzle and clown's face activities with the teacher.

Preparation Directions for Puzzle:

1. Mount the puzzle page on a piece of poster board.

2. Cut the puzzle pieces apart.

3. Place the puzzle pieces in a hose box.

4. Print these directions on the inside cover of the box.

   Draw one piece of the puzzle. Read the directions on the puzzle piece and write the words on a piece of paper. Place the puzzle piece on a top of a desk. Continue to draw puzzle pieces, read the directions on them and write the words on a piece of paper. When the puzzle is completed, ask the teacher to check the puzzle and the words.

Preparation Directions for the Clown's Face:

1. Mount the clown's face on a piece of poster board and cover it with clear contact paper.

2. Cut out the "cheek doors" on the clown's face.

3. Print twenty definitions on pieces of poster board that will fit inside the "cheek door" labeled "definitions."

4. Provide twenty squares of poster board the same size as the definition cards.

5. Place the definition cards in the bottom of a hose box and the blank cards beside the box.

6. Instruct students to reach inside the "definition door" and take a definition card and write the vocabulary word for the definition on a blank card.

7. Place the vocabulary word card in the "word door."

8. Continue until all the definition cards have been drawn and the vocabulary words have been written.

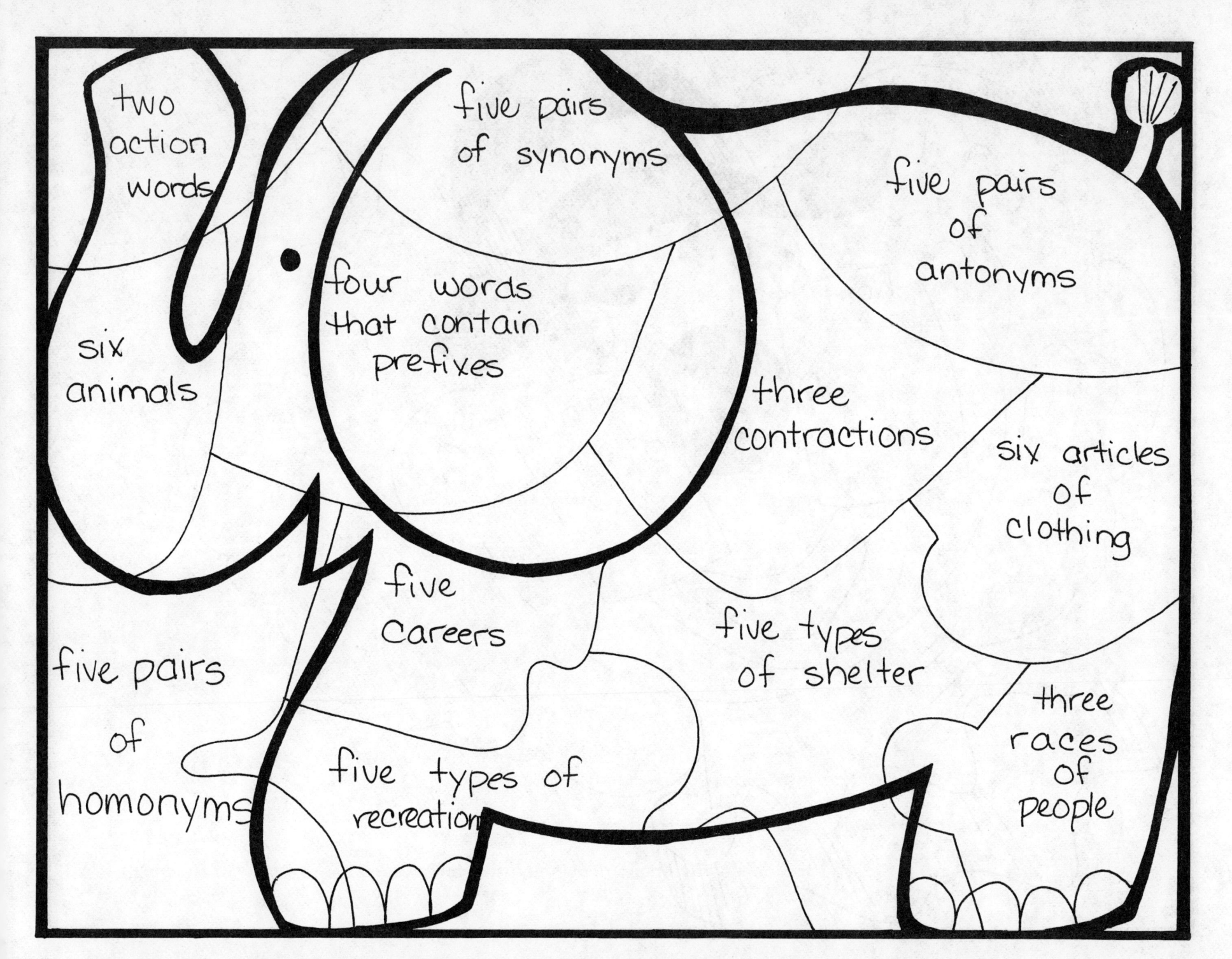

- two action words
- five pairs of synonyms
- five pairs of antonyms
- six animals
- four words that contain prefixes
- three contractions
- six articles of clothing
- five careers
- five types of shelter
- five pairs of homonyms
- five types of recreation
- three races of people

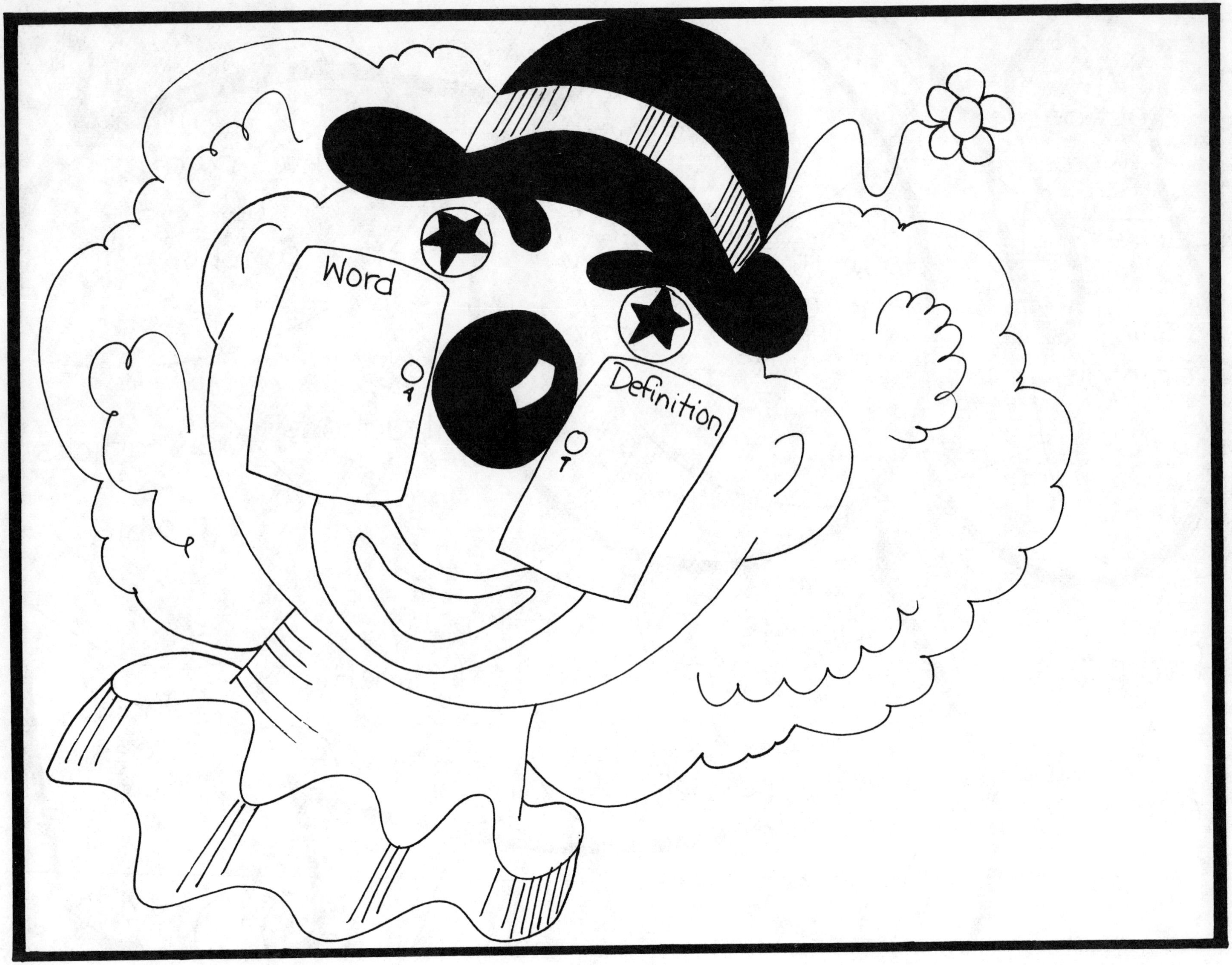
Word
Definition

Jaunty Jargon

Preparation Directions:

1. Reproduce copies of the Jaunty Jargon activity sheets on the following pages.

2. Provide pencils, newspapers and CB dictionaries for the students.

3. Print the student directions on a chart or task card if the activity is to be used in a learning center or other independent setting. If used as a group activity or an individually guided student project, the directions may be given orally.

4. Discuss the concept of jargon with students. Reinforce their understanding by encouraging students to supply examples of jargon with which they are familiar.

Student Directions:

1. Read the directions on each of the Jaunty Jargon activity sheets very carefully before you begin to write. Some jargon is so commonly used that we forget it is jargon. Take your time to be sure you don't miss any of the terms.

2. Use a dictionary for help if you need it.

3. Discuss your completed work with the teacher.

Specialized language is called jargon. Sports jargon is often used by many people. Take a sports jargon quiz and see how you score! Read each word and list the sport in which the jargon term would be used.

tackle _____	double fault _____
spare _____	jack knife _____
swan dive _____	fast break _____
lobbed _____	birdie _____
face-off _____	lap _____
safety _____	grand slam _____
goalie _____	touchdown _____

double play _____

Sports Jargon

Read the sports section of the newspaper. Write the jargon terms that you find in the paper.

_____ _____ _____ _____ _____

_____ _____ _____ _____ _____

Write an article about your favorite sport for the newspaper. Underline each jargon term.

CBer's have their very own jargon, and many of their terms have become widely known and used. Take the CB test below to see how much of their language you already know. Use a CB dictionary if you need help.

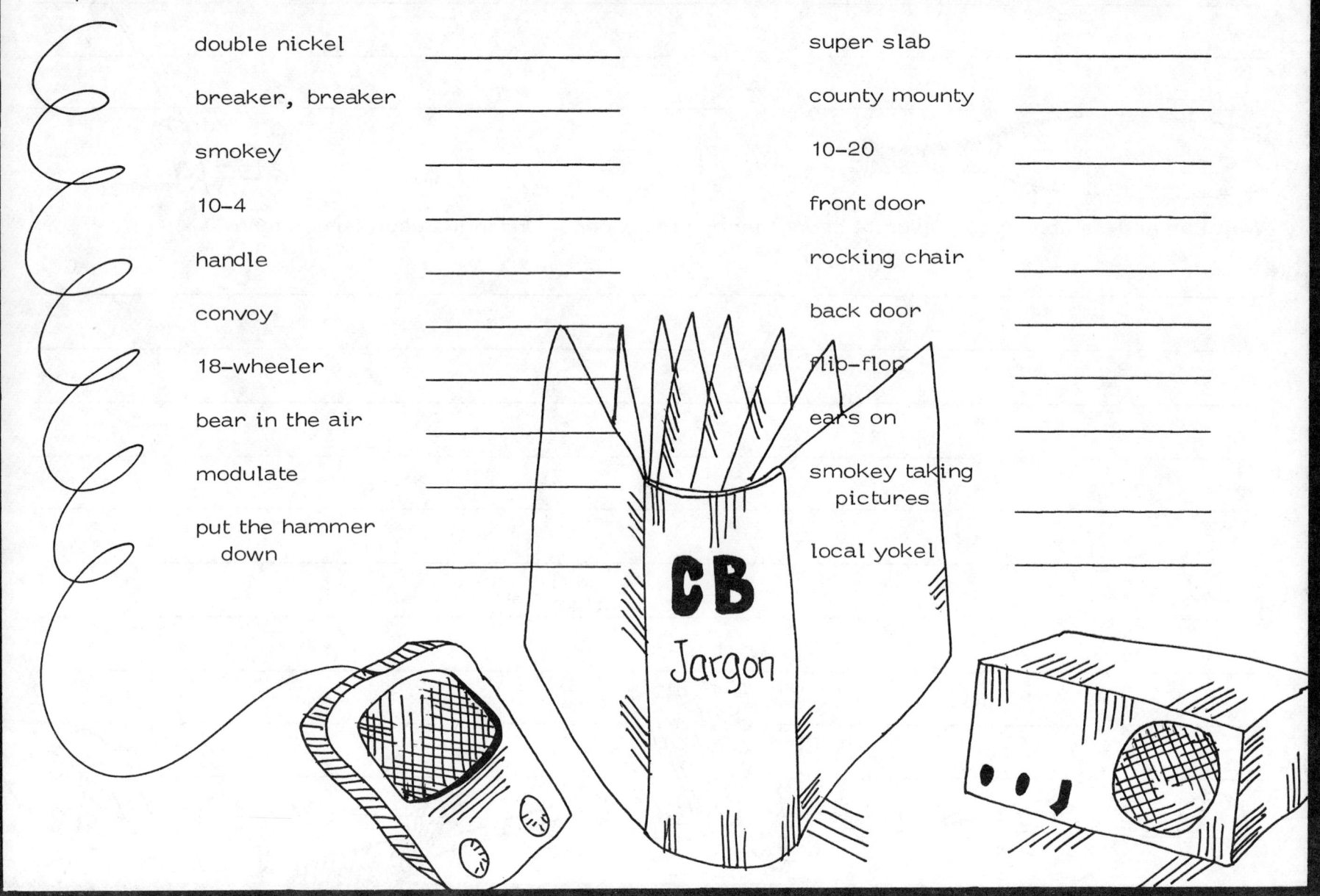

double nickel	_____	super slab	_____
breaker, breaker	_____	county mounty	_____
smokey	_____	10-20	_____
10-4	_____	front door	_____
handle	_____	rocking chair	_____
convoy	_____	back door	_____
18-wheeler	_____	flip-flop	_____
bear in the air	_____	ears on	_____
modulate	_____	smokey taking pictures	_____
put the hammer down	_____	local yokel	_____

CB Jargon

Picture Premium

Preparation Directions:

1. Reproduce copies of the Picture Premium activity sheets on the following pages.

2. Provide pencils, paste, scissors, crayons, poster board and colored construction paper.

3. Print the student directions on a chart or task card if the activity is to be used in a learning center or other independent setting. If used as a group activity or an individually guided student project, the directions may be given orally.

Student Directions:

1. Read the directions or ask the teacher to read the directions on each activity sheet before you begin.

2. Discuss your completed work with the teacher.

doll

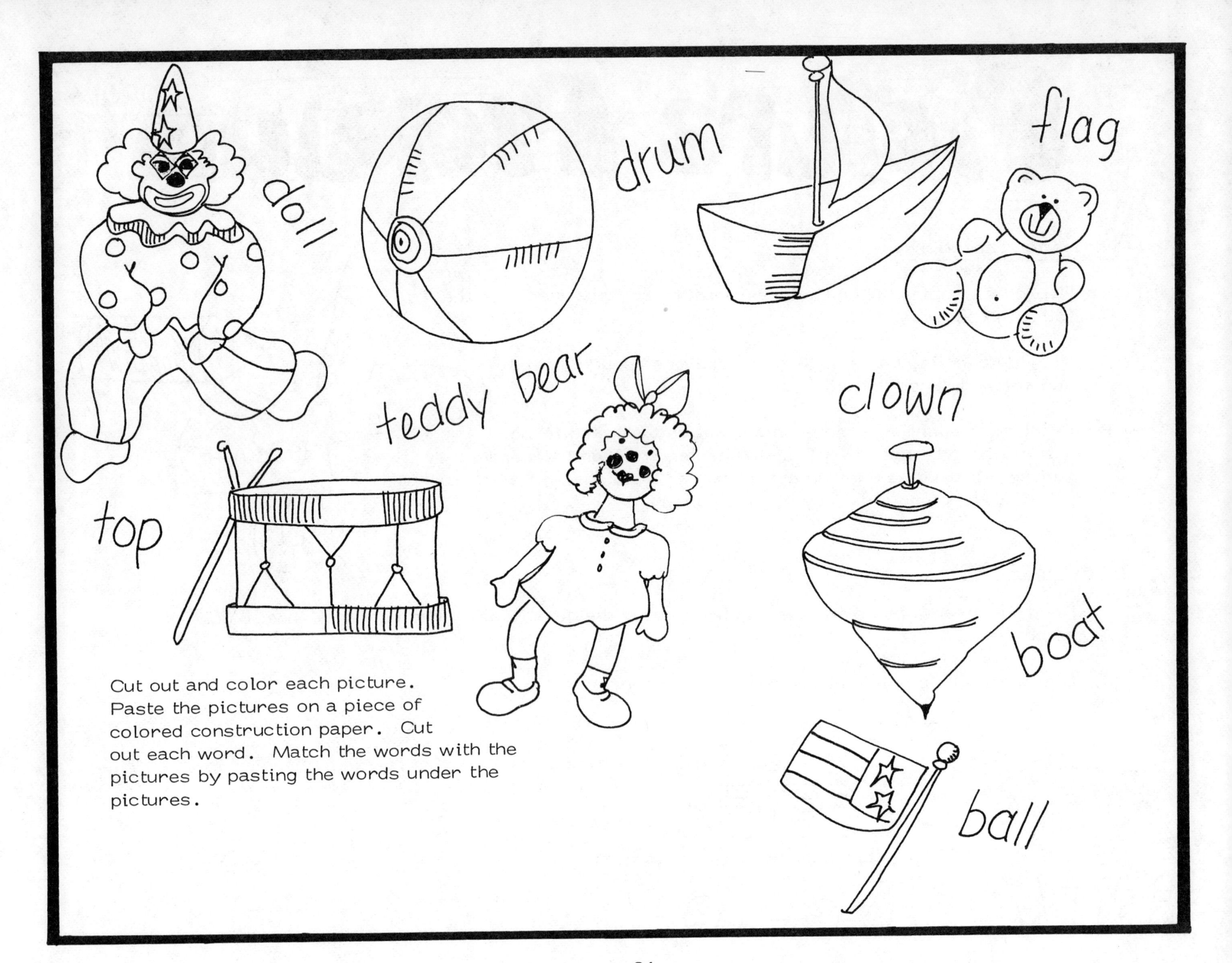

drum

flag

teddy bear

clown

top

boat

ball

Cut out and color each picture. Paste the pictures on a piece of colored construction paper. Cut out each word. Match the words with the pictures by pasting the words under the pictures.

School

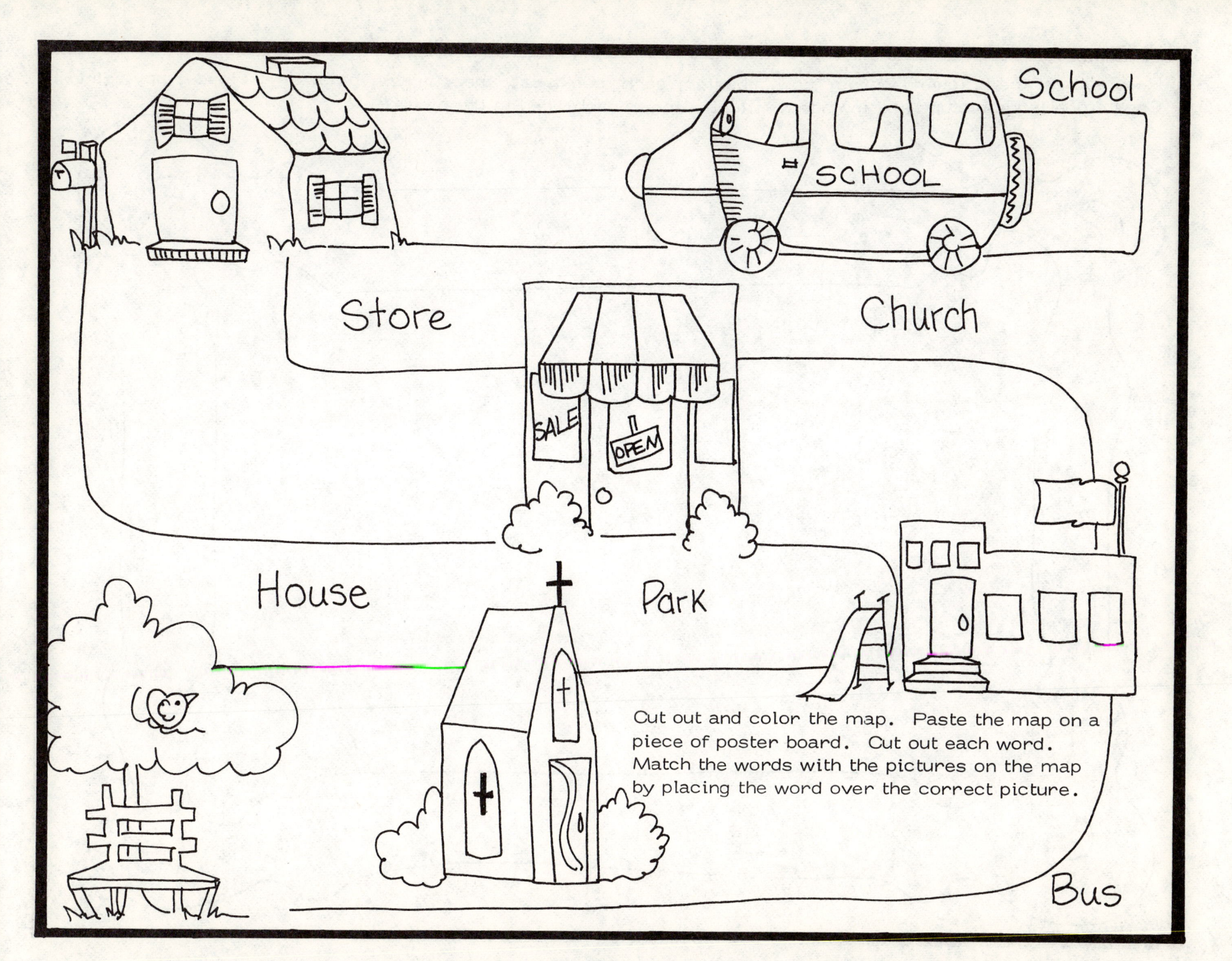

Store

Church

House

Park

Cut out and color the map. Paste the map on a piece of poster board. Cut out each word. Match the words with the pictures on the map by placing the word over the correct picture.

Bus

85

Read each of the following words: cow, rooster, barn, duck, cat, tree, grass, gate, sky, clouds, boy, girl. Create one large picture and include an illustration of each word in the picture.

Prefix Preview

Preparation Directions:

1. Reproduce copies of the Prefix Preview activity sheets on the following pages.

2. Provide dictionaries, pencils and writing paper.

3. Print the student directions on a chart or task card if the activity is to be used in a learning center or other independent setting. If used as a group activity or an individually guided student project, the directions may be given orally.

4. Discuss and review previous work with prefixes.

5. Ask students to assist in listing commonly used prefixes on a chart or on the chalkboard.

Student Directions:

1. Read the directions on each of the Prefix Preview activity sheets very carefully before you begin to write. Try to imagine that you are actually viewing a television program as you complete the activities.

2. Use your dictionary or other resource books for help if you need it.

3. Discuss your completed work with the teacher.

The Prefix Preview opens today and only students who are interested in prefixes will be invited. Each guest is asked to bring thirty words that contain prefixes as the ticket of admission. Write the words that you will use as your ticket.

The Prefix Preview Premier will feature "Prefixes on Parade." Draw stick people to illustrate the prefixes. For the body of each stick person, write a prefix. Add and color facial expressions, hair, hands and feet. Include scenery and stage props.

Draw pictures showing how people attending the Prefix Preview might feel if the performance does not live up to their expectations.

impatient	disenchanted	uninterested	misinformed
displeased	dissatisfied	unfulfilled	unhappy

Sea Breeze

Preparation Directions:

1. Reproduce copies of the Sea Breeze scene and activity sheets on the following pages.

2. Provide dictionaries, pencils, writing paper, colored construction paper, paste, plastic kitchen wrap and scissors.

3. Print the student directions on a chart or task card if the activity is to be used in a learning center or other independent setting. If used as a group activity or an individually guided student project, the directions may be given orally.

Student Directions:

1. Look very carefully at the Sea Breeze scene. Note as many details as possible.

2. Circle pictures of sixteen objects that have compound word names.

3. List the compound words on the Sea Breeze work sheet. (Use the dictionary for correct spelling of any words of which you are uncertain.)

4. Beside each word write the two words that make up the compound word.

5. In the third column, write the plural form of the compound word. If the plural and the singular forms are the same, write "same" in the column.

6. Follow the directions on the remaining Sea Breeze activity sheet.

7. Share the suspense stories with the class.

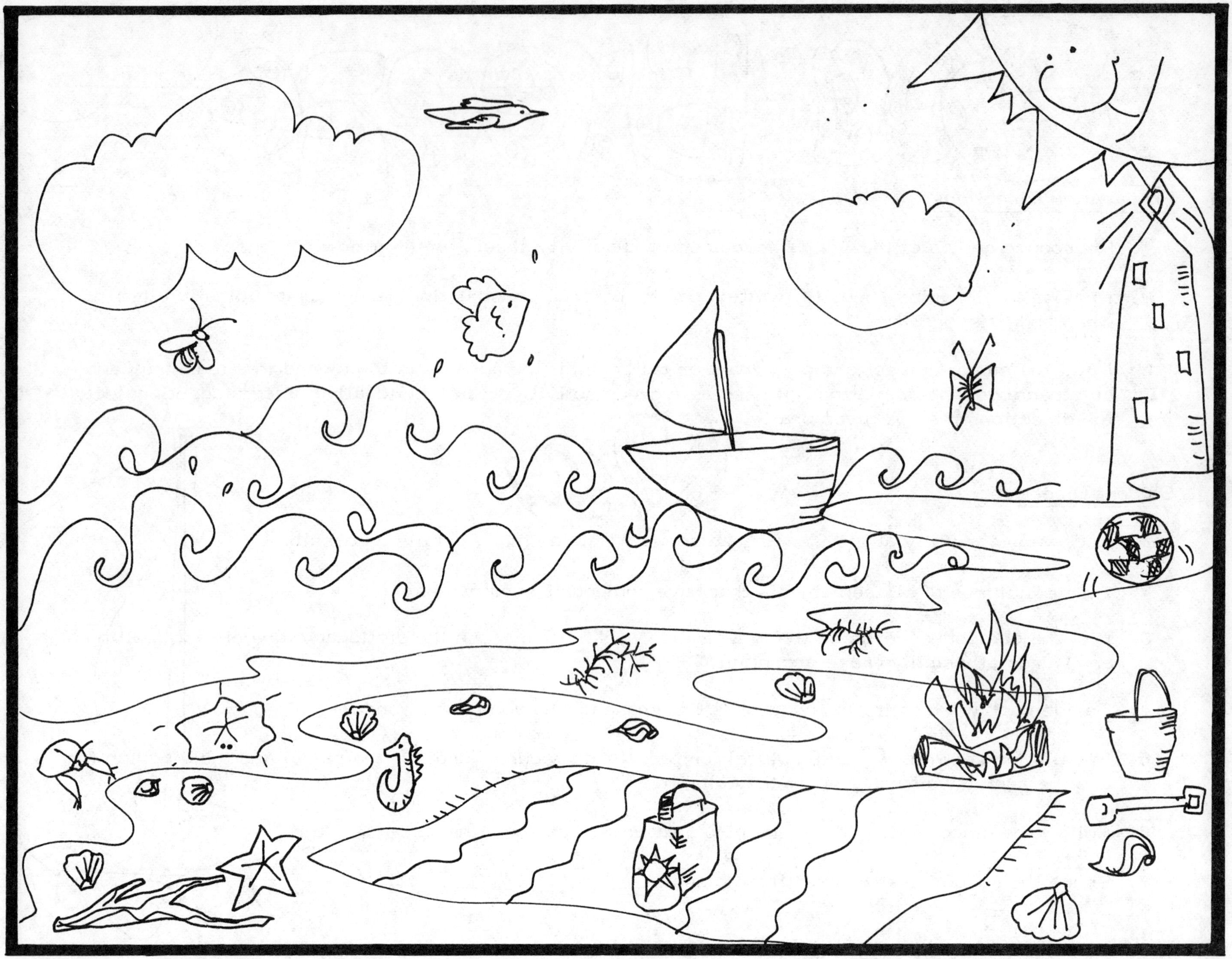

Compound Word　　　　　　　　　Components (two words)　　　　　　　　　Plural Form

Use the Sea Breeze scene as the setting for an original suspense story. Use at least half of the compound words found in the scene and five or more additional ones in the story. Select three or more of your classmates to be the main characters in the story. Mount your story on a piece of blue construction paper. Paste clear plastic kitchen wrap over the picture. Create an underwater scene by cutting out objects from colored construction paper and pasting them on the plastic wrap.

Synonym Sample

Preparation Directions:

1. Tape one activity and reproduce copies of the Synonym Sample activity sheets on the following pages.

2. Provide colored construction paper, writing paper and pencils.

3. Print the student directions on a chart or task card if the activity is to be used in a learning center or other independent setting. If used as a group activity or an individually guided student project, the directions may be given orally.

4. Discuss and review previous work with synonyms.

5. Ask students to assist in listing commonly used synonyms on a chart or on the chalkboard.

Student Directions:

1. Read the directions on each of the Synonym Sample activity sheets very carefully before you begin.

2. Listen carefully to the tape and write a synonym for each word indicated by the ringing bell.

3. Discuss your completed work with the teacher.

A thesaurus is a book of words. Make your own thesaurus of synonyms. Divide the thesaurus into three parts: easy synonyms, difficult synonyms and challenging synonyms. Use a resource book if you need help. Design a cover for the thesaurus using colored construction paper.

Easy Synonyms	Difficult Synonyms	Challenging Synonyms
_____	_____	_____
_____	_____	_____
_____	_____	_____
_____	_____	_____
_____	_____	_____
_____	_____	_____
_____	_____	_____
_____	_____	_____

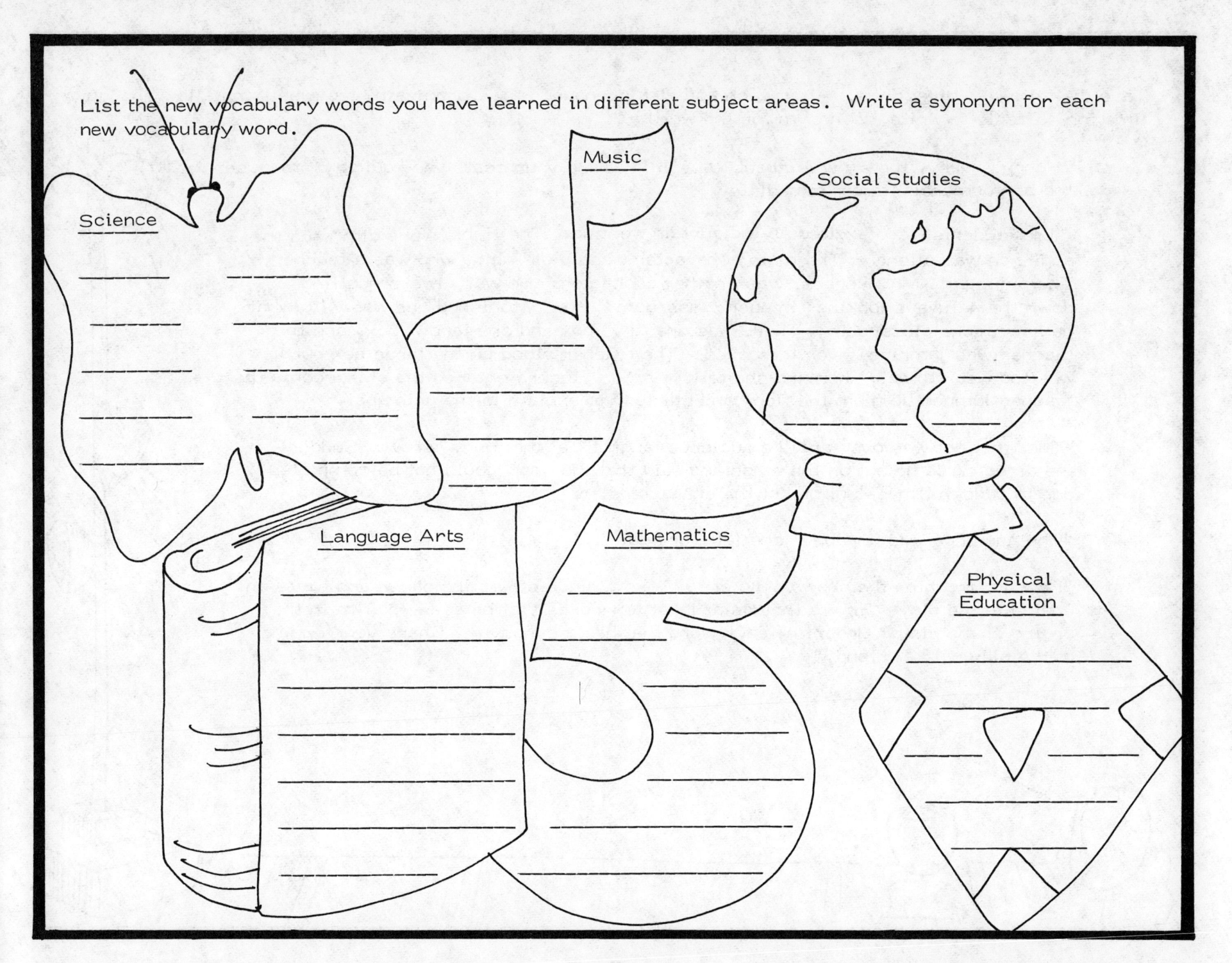

List the new vocabulary words you have learned in different subject areas. Write a synonym for each new vocabulary word.

Science

Music

Social Studies

Language Arts

Mathematics

Physical Education

Tape the following directions. After each asterisk pronounce the word again, tap a bell and allow enough time for students to write a synonym for the word.

"Hurry, hurry, the show is about to begin*! Take your seats very quickly* because the performance starts immediately*.

"The students were excited as the curtain went up. The lights were dim* and the audience was silent*. The main* character was an old* lady who was a teacher. The principal, Mr. Rogers, was another character. He was always hustling* down the hallways looking* in each classroom. How astonished* he was with what he saw in one classroom! There was one tiny* box and one large* box, and the teacher was jumping* over the boxes. The teacher stood on the large box but it was too weak to hold* her and she fell. As Mr. Rogers entered the classroom, the teacher jumped up from the floor and started* to explain to the principal.

"The first act was over and the audience laughed* at the funny* show. Suddenly the director came out on the stage and said that the show could not be completed* due to sudden illness* of one of the characters.

"The audience was unhappy* and left very quietly*.

"How do you think the show would end? Take a piece of writing paper and write an ending to the play. Try to include at least ten words that have a synonym in the ending of the play. Underline each word that has a synonym. Share your ending of the play with a friend."

Valuable Values

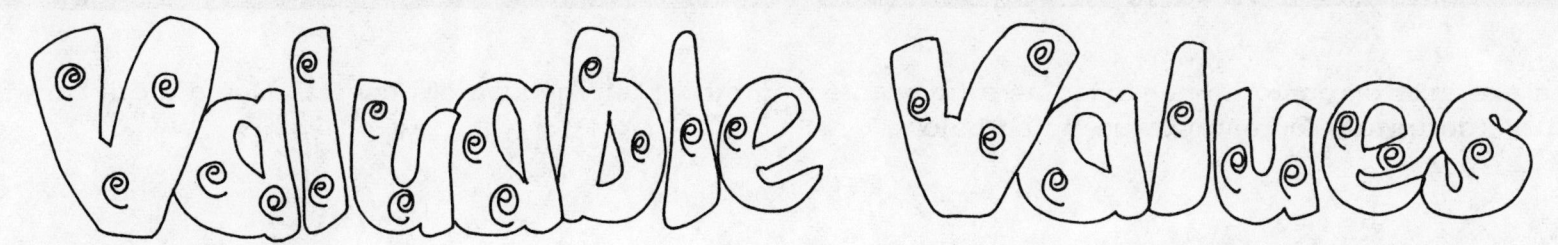

Preparation Directions:

1. Reproduce copies of the Valuable Values activity sheets on the following pages.

2. Provide dictionaries, writing paper, pencils and crayons.

3. Print the student directions on a chart or task cards if the activity is to be used in a learning center or other independent setting. If used as a group activity or individually guided student project, the directions may be given orally.

4. Provide books on values and allow time for students to read them.

5. Discuss values in small groups or one large group.

Student Directions:

1. Read the directions on each of the Valuable Values activity sheets very carefully before you begin.

2. Discuss your completed work with the teacher.

Values are acts or customs regarded as a favorable way by certain groups of people. Use a dictionary to write a definition for each value listed below.

Affection _____
_____

Enlightenment _____
_____

Power _____
_____

Rectitude _____
_____

Respect _____
_____

Skill _____
_____

Wealth _____
_____

Show a pictorial example of each of the values listed below. Write a caption above each illustration explaining the picture.

Affection	Enlightenment	Power	Rectitude

Respect	Skill	Wealth	Well-being

Circle all the words that are related to values. Write all of the words that you found in the puzzle on the lines beside the puzzle and on the back of the activity page.

a	b	i	l	i	t	y	m	o	r	a	l	a	w	p	v
h	r	c	o	n	c	e	r	n	e	d	k	u	t	r	u
u	o	q	v	y	h	v	i	g	o	r	m	t	s	o	r
s	a	n	e	g	o	w	c	l	f	o	z	h	o	p	q
d	t	n	o	a	n	o	h	a	p	p	y	o	n	e	m
e	o	c	j	r	e	r	e	a	s	o	n	r	l	r	s
m	r	e	d	n	s	d	s	t	p	h	o	i	k	t	t
w	a	n	t	b	t	v	j	u	d	g	e	t	f	y	r
t	i	u	x	c	y	e	s	t	e	e	m	y	o	h	e
k	r	t	c	h	a	r	a	c	t	e	r	i	r	g	n
t	h	p	r	i	n	c	i	p	l	e	s	j	c	f	g
p	o	s	s	e	s	s	i	o	n	s	t	v	e	e	t
x	h	p	a	i	n	f	l	u	e	n	c	e	c	d	h

_____
_____
_____
_____
_____
_____
_____
_____
_____
_____
_____
_____
_____

102

Word Foolers

Preparation Directions:

1. Reproduce copies of the Word Foolers activity sheets on the following pages.

2. Provide pencils and lists of vocabulary words for each student.

3. Print the student directions on a chart or task card if the activity is to be used in a learning center or other independent setting. If used as a group activity or an individually guided student project, the directions may be given orally.

4. Discuss various word games, especially scrambled words and rebus games.

Student Directions:

1. Read the directions on each Word Foolers activity sheet very carefully before you begin. Word games are more fun if they are difficult, so try to make your games difficult.

2. Check your spelling by using your vocabulary word list.

3. Discuss your completed work with the teacher.

Have fun with words! Make a list of any of your new reading vocabulary words. In the next column scramble the words. Cover the vocabulary words and ask a friend to unscramble the words and write them in the third column.

New Vocabulary Words   Scrambled Words   Unscrambled Words

Try this with words! Make a list using new vocabulary words. These words can be from language arts, mathematics, social studies or science. In the second column leave out one, two or three letters and write the remaining letters.

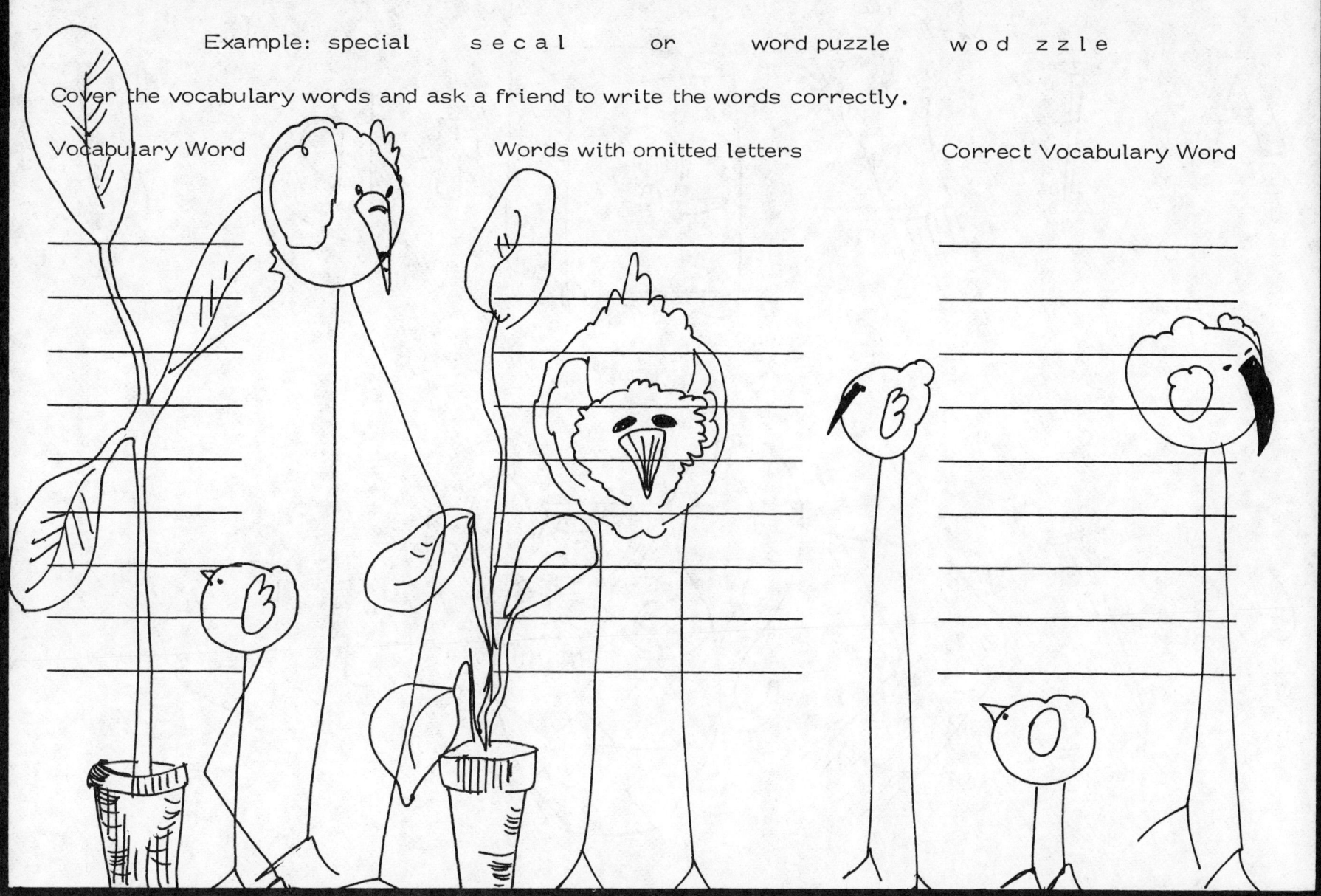

Example: special   s e c a l   or   word puzzle   w o d   z z l e

Cover the vocabulary words and ask a friend to write the words correctly.

Vocabulary Word   Words with omitted letters   Correct Vocabulary Word

A rebus is a puzzle consisting of pictures, signs, phonetic sounds, phrases or words. Read the following rebus and then write one of your own on the back of this activity page. Mount the rebus that you write on a piece of colored construction paper and display it on the bulletin board.

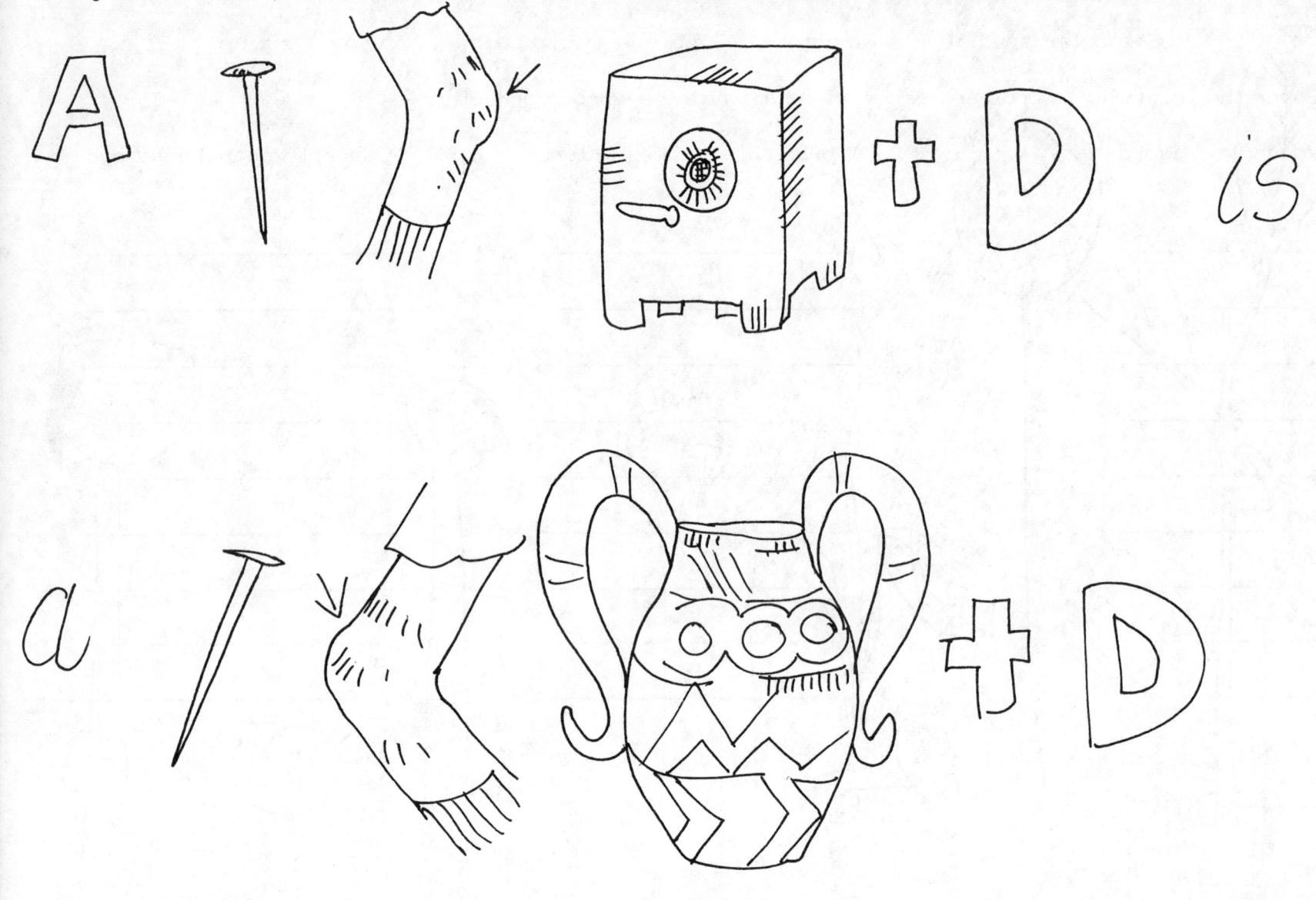

Wonderful Words

Preparation Directions:

1. Reproduce copies of the Wonderful Words activity sheets on the following pages.

2. Provide dictionaries, pencils, writing paper, index cards and crayons.

3. Print the student directions on a chart or task card if the activity is to be used in a learning center or other independent setting. If used as a group activity or an individually guided student project, the directions may be given orally.

4. Discuss and review multiple meanings of words.

Student Directions:

1. Read the directions on each of the Wonderful Words activity sheets very carefully before you begin.

2. Use the dictionary or other resource books for help if you need it.

3. Discuss your completed work with the teacher.

Turn the television on and select the channel that is airing "Wonderful Words." The station seems to be experiencing technical difficulty and this message is being shown on the screen:

During the short delay of "Wonderful Words" you are asked to prepare yourself for the program by listing all the words you can think of that have more than one meaning. Use a dictionary if you need help in finding words.

_____   _____   _____

_____   _____   _____

_____   _____   _____

_____   _____   _____

_____   _____   _____

_____   _____   _____

"Wonderful Words" is a weekly television program that helps build vocabulary. The announcer is asking each viewer to write sentences using two meanings for each word and submit them to the television station.

nap _____
_____

yards _____
_____

pen _____
_____

well _____
_____

watch _____
_____

nag _____
_____

ground _____
_____

On each "Wonderful Words" television program, directions for making a game are given. Follow the directions and make your own card game.

1. You will need twenty index cards.

2. Think of ten words that have more than one meaning.

3. Draw and color a picture on two cards to show two meanings of one word.

4. Make a design on the back of each card.

The following playing directions were given on the television program. You can follow these directions and play the game, or you can make up your own directions for playing the game.

1. Ask a classmate to play the game with you.

2. Shuffle and deal all the cards.

3. If there are two cards that have the same picture word meaning, place them on the table.

4. The first player draws a card from the other player.

5. If the card that was drawn makes a "book", the player places the cards on the table.

6. If the card that was drawn does not make a book, the player keeps the card.

7. Continue to play until all the cards have been matched.

8. The player with the most books wins the game.

Notes

it's magic

the Basic Skills Magic-Mastery Series

Each book in this series presents a unique, well-organized, high-interest collection of creative games, puzzles, quizzes and pupil-centered activities for extending and enriching basic skills. Each set of duplicating masters presents a variety of visually exciting pupil-ready independent activity pages for reinforcing one or more basic skills.

IDEA BOOKS

SPELLING MAGIC

METRIC MAGIC

VOCABULARY MAGIC

COMPREHENSION MAGIC

DUPLICATING MASTERS

SPELLING MASTERY

METRIC MASTERY

VOCABULARY MASTERY

COMPREHENSION MASTERY